Patterns of Ministry

Steven Mackie # Patterns of Ministry

*Theological Education in a
Changing World*

with a foreword by
Dr. W. A. Visser 't Hooft

COLLINS   *St James's Place, London 1969*

SBN 00 215671 7

Printed in Great Britain by
C. Tinling & Co. Ltd,
London and Prescot

Contents

Foreword

There are few churches left in which the nature and form of the ministry are not being questioned. There are even fewer theological faculties or colleges left in which students and professors are not engaged in a search for new patterns of ministry.

At such a moment it is important that the discussion be set in the right context. That context is in our time surely a world-wide and ecumenical context. We cannot rightly understand why traditional concepts of the ministry are no longer adequate unless we recognize the spiritual and social historical forces which operate in all parts of the world and create a new unprecedented situation for the Church.

The significance of this book is first of all that it provides such a world-dimension for the discussion concerning the future shape of the ministry. It is based on a process of study, discussion and dialogue in which men and women of churches in all continents have participated and which has taken three years. It is a mine of information for all who are concerned about this decisive issue for the life and mission of the Church. No one can read it with an open mind without receiving new light on the subject.

This is furthermore an encouraging book. The discussion concerning the ministry is often carried out in a gloomy atmosphere. The emphasis is all too often on the disintegration of the long-established patterns or on the unwillingness of a new generation to accept the traditional structures. The men who have worked on this study and their spokesman Steven Mackie do not speak in these tones of defeatism. They accept the fact that old doors are being closed, but concentrate their attention on new doors which are being opened. They

7

show that already in many places new patterns of ministry are beginning to take shape. They add their own suggestions concerning the direction of advance. What is offered is not a definitive blueprint— no one can give this today—but 'grist for the mill', stimulating ideas concerning new possibilities and opportunities.

It is obvious that this book should be read by church leaders and theological educators. But I hope that it will also reach many church members who are wondering about the shape which the life of the Church should take in the coming decades. For in the last resort the renewal of the pattern of ministry will not take place unless the whole people of God discover that faithfulness has nothing to do with lack of imagination and immobilism, but everything to do with the following of the guidance of the Holy Spirit toward a future in which there will be new opportunities and new forms of Christian obedience.

W. A. Visser 't Hooft

Introduction

At a time when all institutions are being widely questioned, the institutions of the Christian Church cannot remain unscathed. Chief among the institutions which are shaken is the professional ministry. Ministers, laymen and theological students are asking searching questions, both about the ministry itself, and about the training which ministers receive. To take one example, in the city of Geneva, twenty-two younger ministers recently addressed a manifesto to the authorities of the National Protestant Church. This manifesto challenged official statements about the doctrine of the ministry and affirmed the intention of its authors to refuse ordination and all it meant, because of the distinction made between ministers and laymen in the Church.

'We are convinced', they said, 'that the ministry of the Church is fulfilled in the ministry of every church-member. It is wrong to isolate one particular ministry (the pastoral ministry) and to give it special privileges because it exercises functions which are claimed to be essential (preaching, administration of the sacraments, teaching, the cure of souls etc.).

For these reasons we request the authorities of the Church:

1. to modify Section VI of the Church's Constitution . . .
2. to take the steps necessary to permit us to serve Jesus Christ as a community according to our individual capacities and in relation to the basic needs of contemporary society'.[1]

This is only one example among many. It is characteristic of a time when a new generation is challenging structures inherited from the past. But it is not just a case of student intransigence opposed to institutional inflexibility. The situation is quite different. The frustration of students and younger ministers is shared by many who have responsibility for theological education and for theological reflection in the churches. This widespread challenge comes at a time when many churches are already engaged in rethinking their views on the ministry, in the light of ecumenical discussion on the mission of the Church and on the ministry of the laity. At the same time, in many cases, churches and theological schools are seriously reconsidering the traditional structure and content of theological education in the light of new thinking about education and about theology. Changes are beginning to be made.

In 1961, the New Delhi Assembly of the World Council of Churches called for an ecumenical enquiry on the training of the ministry. This was set up in 1964 as a Study on Patterns of Ministry and Theological Education, with the present writer as Executive Secretary. The aim of the study was to look at the theological education of ministers in the light of reflection about the ordained ministry and of recent and future changes in the work which ministers do. Much of this reflection stems from the current concern for the ministry of the laity, and yet it was not at first envisaged that the Study should go into that field. It soon became clear, however, that ministry and laity would require a great deal of disentangling. Terms like 'the ministry', 'a professional ministry', 'the ordained ministry' are all equivocal, and they do not necessarily mean the same thing. Later on it also became apparent that 'theological education' could not be discussed without raising the issue of 'laity training'.

This book attempts to describe the progress of an ecumenical study. Part I, on 'Patterns of Ministry', is concerned with the changes in the work of ministers, mentioned above. Inevitably, it also discusses the function of the ministry, the meaning of ordination and the relation between professional ministers and other members of the Church. Part II, on 'Theological Education', describes current thinking and recent experiments in the training of professional ministers. It also discusses the larger subject of the education of the whole people of God. The writer has come to two basic convictions as a result of this study. The first of these is that the churches cannot afford to ignore the current questioning of traditional patterns of ministry and theological education, but must regard it as one of the ways in which God is speaking to his Church. And the second conviction is that neither ministry nor theological education can ultimately be discussed except in terms of the service and formation of all Christians, clergy and laity alike.

To raise an issue is not to solve a problem. The World Council of Churches' Study leaves many problems unsolved. The most it can claim to do is to lead the discussion on the ministry and on theological education into new lines which will have to be carefully pursued. It has seemed to those who have been involved in this Study, that the churches and theological institutions are only beginning to raise the basic issues. A more thorough and a more ecumenical study of the biblical doctrine of the ministry and of its historical evolution is certainly required. But, even more than this, careful consideration is needed of what God is doing with his Church today. Again, theological education demands research into more efficient means of educating ministers in particular attitudes and for particular tasks. But a more basic reflection is also demanded on the kind of community which the Church should be, and the part education can play in preparing Christians for life and ministry within that community.

This book is not a co-operative effort, nor is it an official report. As Secretary of the Study I could not indeed have written it if the Study had not taken place. Few of the ideas are my own, but I have woven them into a whole which is my own creation. I gratefully acknowledge everything I have borrowed from others, at the same time begging the lenders' pardon for the distortion to which their loans have been subject.

The official Report of the Study to the Fourth Assembly of the World Council of Churches at Uppsala, July 1968, is printed as an appendix at the end of the book in the form in which it appears in the Assembly *Work Book*. This Report contains the Recommendations of the World Consultation on Theological Education held at Northwood, near London, in July 1967. The full account of that meeting is contained in the December 1967 issue of *Study Encounter*, available from the World Council of Churches' Publications Department.

STEVEN G. MACKIE

Geneva, 3 January 1969

Part One

Patterns of Ministry

1 · Inherited Patterns of Ministry

The patterns of ministry which we have today are inherited from the past. This is at the same time their strength and their weakness. It is their strength, because in the past they have worked well, and it is easier to continue a good thing than to create a new one equally good. It is their weakness because today is not like the past. The changes even in Western society have been enormous since the days of our grandfathers. In developing societies they have been even greater in less than half the time. If society and its needs have changed, the churches, in ministering to these needs, must surely also change.

Let us think for a moment of these changes as they have affected the life of men in one part of the industrial West, in Scotland where, as it happens, both my grandfathers were ministers over eighty years ago. The mining community where one of them worked is now in large measure a residential suburb of Glasgow; the social and economic problems of that day belong to the past. In the slum area of Edinburgh, on the edge of the New Town, where my other grandfather was minister, many of the houses are still standing, but the social degradation, the drunkenness, the extreme poverty with which my grandfather struggled and about which he wrote are not such pressing problems today. More important perhaps, the activities and interests of the people have widened, their hopes and aspirations have changed. As few books may be read perhaps—and the stories of the Bible are certainly less familiar—but the TV screen brings new ideas and pictures for the mind, and the Sunday sermon seems out-of-date.

If this is true of the world, should it not also be true of the Church? If it is true of the men and women who make up the Church, must it not also be true for their ministers? Can the work of the minister today be quite the same as it was in the past? In the days before the telephone,[1] for instance, a minister could spend all his mornings in his study working at his Sunday sermons, secure in the knowledge that he would be undisturbed since all visitors to the manse must come on foot. How many ministers are in this situation today? Granted that certain elements in the ministry, certain fundamental tasks remain the same, much has already changed. Can we be sure that the patterns of ministry we have inherited from the past are the right ones for the future?

Before trying to answer these questions, we must look at these inherited patterns to see what they are, and how we came by them. There are many such patterns, and not just one, though some writers seem to speak of an unalterable pattern sacred from the time of the New Testament until now. There is a diversity of patterns, and I am not thinking here so much of denominational diversity but of other kinds of diversity which we might call (a) geographical, (b) ecclesiastical and (c) functional.

There is, in the first place, *geographical* diversity. Patterns of ministry vary with the social, physical and economic background of a particular community. In a suburban church in North America, the minister spends a lot of time in administering church organizations, in community involvement, and, if he has the gift, in spiritual counselling. In a rural pastorate in Africa, the pastor is constantly travelling, visiting remote congregations for sacramental services, occasional teaching and pastoral care. The work of the minister varies according to the type of community, the geographical spread, the financial resources available, the educational level and the incidence of special problems such as inter-group conflict, drug-addiction, availability or lack of welfare services, use of different languages and the like. In each of these situations a different pattern of ministry is possible and appropriate, and there is much similarity of pattern between different denominations working in the same situation and between essentially similar situations in different parts

16

of the world. It is for this reason that discussion takes place so easily between ministers of different churches caught up in the same situation. Patterns of ministry appropriate in scattered communities in Africa may also work in the prairie provinces of Canada. Methods of training for urban ministry developed in Chicago, are used with profit by churches in Bangkok.

In addition to this geographical diversity, there is a second kind of diversity which might be termed *ecclesiastical*, since it depends on the structure of the Church and its relation to society. This is clearly related to denominational factors but not exclusively so. In the European scene, for example, the differences between Lutheran, Reformed and Anglican parishes belonging to the national or established churches are much less than those between established or majority churches and minority churches of the same tradition. In Reformed Switzerland as in Lutheran Scandinavia or Germany, in the Church of England or the Church of Scotland, the parish pastor (like the Roman Catholic priest in Italy or Spain and the Orthodox priest in Greece) will have certain civil functions devolving upon him which take up a good part of his time; he may also have other informal functions arising from his position in the community. As a compensation, he will find that he is in a stronger position in dealing with the authorities, and that he comes in touch with a lot of people who do not themselves go to church, and may even be welcome as a visitor to their homes. The pastor of a Free Church in northern Europe or of a minority Protestant church in the south has a much less important social role and a much closer relationship to the members of his flock, many more of whom are probably involved in church activities. The same could be said of the Roman Catholic priest in countries with a Protestant majority.

The Parish across the Ages

Here something must be said about the evolution of the parish ministry, since in many churches, of which the Church of Scotland is one example, the parish ministry is not only considered as the norm, but it is generally assumed that it has been inherited unchanged from the past. In fact the parish minister today has a very different role both in society and in the Church from those of his mediaeval and Reformation predecessors. Though in many European communities there is a legal and geographical continuity between the original parishes established in the early Middle Ages and those of today, the communities themselves are very different; so, indeed, are their pastors.

The parish system was founded at a time when the basis of feudal society was also being laid, roughly between the fourth and the tenth centuries, when the Celtic and Teutonic missions were taking Christianity to northern and central Europe. Although in certain areas such as Ireland the expanding Church encountered a pre-feudal society and adopted structures of a quite different kind, in most of Europe it was natural for it to adopt a basically territorial structure. The earliest monastic missionaries were centred on the courts of kings and princes; soon each lesser lord had his resident chaplain too, and eventually made provision for the ministrations of the Church to his successors and their vassals by building a church and establishing a parish with a grant of land. These parishes inevitably took on the same bounds as the fiefs to which they were linked, and so by about the end of the first millennium, the whole of Europe was divided, as it remains to this day, into territorial parishes and the parish became the effective unit of church life. As it turned out, it was a more enduring unit than the diocese, the older and ecclesiastically more important division.

The historical continuity must not blind us to considerable changes which have taken place in the patterns of ministry. The first parish priest was the personal chaplain of a feudal lord and his house. Only gradually did he become the parson (*persona*) of the parish, the representative in a limited geographical area of the Catholic Church. Although in most cases the parish system was not greatly disrupted by the Reformation, the Reformed or Lutheran pastor in northern and central Europe had a somewhat different function to fulfil from his predecessor in mediaeval times. The legal and geographical limits remained the same but the pastor no longer thought of himself as the local agent of a universal organization. Rather he was a minister of the Word of God sent as prophet and pastor to a particular people. His ministry was still a universal ministry in that he was set over them 'whether they would bear or whether they would forbear', he was the pastor of the congregation, in the wider sense of all God's children in that place. It is in these terms that the responsibilities and duties of the Reformed or Lutheran pastor as also of the Anglican incumbent, are, to this day, defined. Interestingly enough the common conception of the parish ministry in the Roman Catholic Church today is not very different.[2]

Since the Reformation a further development has supervened, effectively complicating the situation. As a result partly of the religious divisions of the seventeenth and eighteenth centuries, and partly of the industrial revolution, the urban parish, though persisting as a legal entity, was replaced as the unit of the church life by the Congregation of the faithful—chiefly those who associated themselves with the activities of a particular minister and church building. In certain European countries, as in North America and elsewhere where denominational pluralism exists, congregations of different churches can coincide or overlap geographically. Unless one of these churches retains a sense of territorial responsibility, it is perfectly possible for residents in the area to have no connection, even a potential connection, with any of them. In countries where one church is in a majority position, the situation may be somewhat different on paper, but in urban areas parish boundaries mean very little and parish responsibility is difficult where one parish may house ten or twenty thousand persons or more. In effect this usually means that only those who attend some activity of the local church, or are involved in some official relationship with the pastor, or specifically demand his services, are within the influence of the Church's ministry. In rural areas, the older situation often persists, though here too denominational pluralism may destroy the original concept of the parish.

In North America, the word 'parish' is often used to refer to the local base of the pastoral ministry, when what is meant is essentially a voluntary congregation without territorial limits. The fact that a 'parish church' in the USA may be as large as a European one and is often actively used by a much larger number of people, is not relevant at this point. It is interesting to see how this new situation has affected denominations which in Europe were either minority or majority churches. The largest Protestant bodies in the States come in fact from the English Free Church tradition (Baptist and Methodist). At the other end of the spectrum, so to speak, the Orthodox churches which, in Europe and the Middle East, have a majority pattern, are developing in the USA into denominations like all the rest. In general, in a plural but voluntary situation like that which obtains in the United States, Australia, New Zealand, English-speaking Canada, and some other countries, all churches tend to start equal and the differences between Protestant, Anglican, Roman Catholic and Orthodox patterns of ministry are very much reduced.

In countries where Christianity is a minority faith, the situation is again different, particularly where it is regarded, as in much of Asia and Africa, as a religion imported from the West. In the former 'mission fields' the pattern of ministry established in the last century was based on the foreign missionary, who frequently superintended a large area with many Christian congregations and a large number of trained and untrained helpers. Missionaries have been increasingly replaced by national pastors, but the pattern is often unchanged. This results in an unsatisfactory situation where the pastor has a vast amount of administration, a great many congregations to oversee, from which he is artificially separated both by his position and his education. Happily the situation is changing in many areas. Experiments are being made with 'tent-making ministers' who do not require costly financial support or long training. The number of theological seminaries has greatly increased so that pastors do not need to go abroad to study, and much is being done to relate theological courses to the actual situation of the congregations. Again in countries where missionaries have been banished and foreign support cut off an entirely new situation has been created. Where, as in Indonesia, this has been followed by an influx of new Christians the old patterns of ministry may have to be replaced by something else.

Other situations also exist which have not been mentioned; that of the Church in Muslim countries for instance, or under Communist regimes in Eastern Europe and in China. In some cases new patterns of ministry appear to be developing; in others political oppression or control may actually freeze old patterns, since all change is dangerous, and the churches are least in danger when they change least. As candidates for the ministry tend to be in short supply, the temptation to keep things as they are is strong, but may prove impracticable. One interesting aspect of the situation in the Protestant Churches of Eastern Europe is the much greater use of women as pastors than in related churches in the West.

Enough has been said to indicate that when church leaders extol the parish ministry, or when young pastors confess themselves at a loss how to act within its structures, they are speaking not of an unchanging and unalterable system handed down from the earliest period of the Church, or even from Reformation times, but of a varied and developing sociological structure which has different characteristics today from what it had in the past, and from one European country and church to another. There is no place in Church history, and still less in Scripture, for a concept of the parish and ministry binding for all time and in every place. This is not to say that the faith of the Church, and its life in obedience to the commands of God, do not require as a permanent feature the gathering together in congregations with a local and temporal expression as well as a pastoral, preaching and liturgical ministry. But though a congregation must have a certain enduring quality and must gather both in and from a certain place and at a certain time, it clearly need not have a continued legal existence over many centuries nor be tied to a particular area excluding other such areas. Again, though a minister may normally be called to exercise his ministry in relation to such a congregation, this does not mean that his rights and duties must be defined in terms of a territorial parish or of a legal corporation.

In a later chapter we shall have to consider suggestions regarding new ways in which the local gathering of the Church might be structured. It is important that experiments of this kind, some of which have already taken place—should be accompanied by serious ecumenical reflection on the relation between the theological basis of the traditional parish and its various historical forms. As things are, those who defend the parish principle to the exclusion of all else claim too much and, for this reason, ignore other equally important aspects of the situation.

An Alternative Pattern?

The parish ministry is not the only pattern inherited from the past. It is here we come to our third kind of diversity, a *functional* diversity. Not all ministers are parish pastors; some of them, like hospital chaplains or theological professors, have 'specialized' functions. Nor is this something entirely new. Even in the mediaeval church many priests—most of them members of monastic orders—were engaged in education, diaconal or administrative work, similar to that done by specialist ministers today.

The churches of the Reformation cut down their number insisting on the primacy of the pastoral ministry. But exceptions were still made, notably for theological professors. By the time of the Wars of Religion, at least, there were military chaplains, and, in a number of churches, some ordained ministers continued to spend most of their time in education and in scholarship. During the eighteenth and nineteenth centuries when, on the whole, there were more than enough ministers in European churches to fill vacant pastorates, a certain number were employed in various specialized capacities in diaconal institutions and in religious societies in some degree independent from the churches.

So far we have been mainly speaking of those traditions in which the parish ministry has always been central. This was not true originally in the British or European Free Churches, whatever may be the case today. In the early Independent and Anabaptist churches there was far more emphasis on the prophetic than on the pastoral ministry. The settled local congregation, where such existed, was not the only focus of the minister's work. He was primarily a preacher, nor was his preaching confined to those living in a certain parish or worshipping in a particular building. In the later Moravian and Methodist movements, there was the same emphasis on evangelism. The pattern of ministry which developed was evangelistic, it was usually non-professional, it was often itinerant. Although there was, of course, great variety—greater variety perhaps than in many settled churches—it was generally true that well on into the nineteenth century this more flexible pattern persisted. It proved particularly successful in fluid situations such as the settlement of the American frontier, where the Free Churches had a head start, only partly overcome by the later settlement of whole communities from northern and central Europe bringing their traditions and their pastors with them. The same point could be made, with even greater force, of patterns of ministry in Latin America today, in some of the most rapidly growing churches in the world.[3]

This *alternative pattern* of ministry has always existed in the Church, alongside the settled pastoral pattern.[4] Such documents of the Early Church as the *Didache* mention in passing the itinerant ministry of prophets which was apparently not assimilated to the presbyterate but which could also claim scriptural authority. With the establishment of Christianity as the official religion of the Empire, the emphasis was naturally placed on the systematic development of a settled pastoral ministry (though one in some respects dissimilar from the parish ministry of a later period). The growth of monasticism, particularly in its Western form, soon provided, however, an alternative pattern of ministry which was to have a long development. In part, at least, this pattern was a missionary pattern—particularly in its early days when missionary monks carried out the Christianization of northern Europe.

A detailed study of this alternative pattern would certainly refer to the emergence in turn of the Dominican and Franciscan Orders; of the Waldensians and Hussites; of the Anabaptists and Independents; of the Society of Jesus; of Pietists and Methodists; of the foreign missionary movement of the eighteenth and nineteenth centuries; of the YMCA, the Salvation Army, Catholic Action and so on. Many, though not all, of these groups had a strong missionary emphasis; some of them were largely of lay initiative; but they all had this in common that they did not depend for their inspiration and guidance on the settled pastoral ministry, and that they provided an outlet for ministers with talents and motivation subtly different from those required in whatever was the current pattern of pastoral ministry. Specialist ministers today belong to the same tradition.

The groups and movements referred to above were mostly of a sectarian nature, in that those belonging to them were members either of separate churches or of particular groups within the total body of Christendom. They might be said to constitute a threat and a challenge to the dominant tradition of the European churches, but it was one that could usually be ignored simply because most Christians, and most Christian pastors, disapproved of such enthusiastic and radical activities. (The attitude of the Roman Catholic Church to the monastic orders was of course more complex.)[5] If the specialized ministries seem today to constitute more of a problem for the churches than did these earlier phases of the alternative pattern it is simply because they are not separate, and it is necessary, therefore, to bring them into some coherent relation with the 'parish ministry'.

2 · Specialist Ministers

What are these specialized ministries? How many specialist ministers are there, and what do they do? In 1964 a questionnaire was sent out to 140 European churches to try and answer these questions. The information received from the Orthodox churches and from Protestant churches in Eastern Europe was extremely scanty, although it was sufficient to conclude that the number of specialist ministers in these churches was very small. The information in Table I (page 163) refers therefore to the 83 churches in Western Europe which replied to the questionnaire (3 Old Catholic Churches, 5 Anglican, 3 Baptist, 5 Methodist, 1 Moravian, 3 Congregational, 5 other Free Churches, 31 Reformed, 27 Lutheran and 8 United, i.e. Reformed-Lutheran). The Roman Catholic Church was not included, nor were those churches which are unrelated to the World Council of Churches, notably, so far as Europe is concerned, the Pentecostal churches.

Each church was asked for the 'total number of its ordained ministers (excluding those working abroad or in complete retirement)', and for the number 'related to local congregations or parishes' on the one hand, and 'responsible for pastoral oversight (e.g. Bishops etc.)', on the other. As regards the remainder, a detailed classification of specialized ministries was suggested, with five main divisions and over twenty sub-divisions, and churches were asked to give the number of ministers in each category, working 'full-time' in a specialized ministry. A full report of the survey was published in 1966 in duplicated form and sent to the churches concerned.

Taking into account certain factors, which made the results only approximate, it is possible to summarize these results briefly as follows:

1. In the 83 churches concerned there were at the end of 1964 some 52,000 'ordained ministers' of whom about 400 were women.

2. About 86·8 per cent of these were engaged in pastoral work in local congregations or in pastoral oversight. This leaves 13·8 per cent, or roughly 6,800 engaged in specialized ministries of different kinds.

3. All the churches replying, with only a few exceptions, recognized the need for some forms of specialized ministry to supplement the traditional patterns of the pastoral ministry.

4. The categories of specialized ministry most strongly represented are those in the education, pastoral and administrative fields; only a small proportion of specialist ministers worked in the field of 'Evangelism and Communication'.

5. In general, those churches with the greatest supply of ministers relative to their size have been most able to develop specialized ministries; the territorial churches with responsibility for a small and highly populated urban area have done this most markedly but certain diaspora churches (some of them with a long tradition of partly non-professional ministry) have a high proportion of ministers in specialist posts.

6. Old Catholic, Reformed and Free Churches have, in general, been more conservative in their use of specialist ministers than have the Anglican, Lutheran and United Churches.

A similar survey conducted in 1965 by Ross P. Scherer of the National Council of the Churches of Christ in the USA, produced comparable statistics which are given in Table II (page 164). These figures relate to 19 out of the 40 Protestant denominations which received his questionnaire. As can be seen from the Table the proportion of specialist ministers is slightly higher than in western Europe.

The detailed breakdown also revealed that in certain churches (notably in the Episcopal Church and in the United Church of Christ) as high as 14 per cent of all ministers were in 'multiple staff parishes', i.e. in congregations with more than one minister. In Europe a pattern of this kind is common in Lutheran parishes in Germany and Scandinavia. No count of these parishes has been taken, but it is unlikely that the percentage is anything like as high as in the States. In Reformed churches in Europe and in the British churches in general, the one-man pattern is far commoner.

A third set of figures is given in Tables III and IV (page 165), for Japan and Korea. It was drawn up as part of the preparation for a consultation on theological education in North East Asia in 1966 and it shows clearly that specialist ministers are not just a Western phenomenon, although the situation of these particular churches is hardly typical, and indeed the figures are not strictly comparable since they refer to seminary graduates rather than to ordained ministers.

A Flight from the Parish?

What are we to make of these figures? Is there, as many have maintained, a 'flight from the parish', either among theological students or among younger ministers? And if so, is there cause for alarm? If we remember that the specialized ministries include theological teaching, church administration and institutional chaplaincies (all of them patterns long sanctioned by tradition) we may feel that a proportion of 1 specialist in 7 ministers in Europe, or 1 in 5 in America, is not excessive. The main cause for concern, perhaps, is not the numbers of men and women so engaged, especially since most of them are in these ministries because their churches have sent them there, but the fact that the churches themselves have not reflected sufficiently on what is happening. Many churches still tend to speak of the 'parish ministry' as the only valid form of professional ministry, and have agreed to the establishment of specialist posts only as exception to a general rule. But 1 in 5, or even 1 in 7, is more than an exception. A policy is required. What is that policy to be? If the matter is left to chance it may well be that the proportion will increase further since in a period of uncertainty the specialized ministries do exert considerable attraction on theological students, and notably on the most imaginative and most able of them, for whom traditional patterns of ministry and church life often seem to be out of date. The work of the specialist appears more clearly defined, his responsibilities more narrowly limited. The structures in this kind of ministry are newer and have less the air of permanence. They appear to require men with particular, specialized gifts. In a day when the increase in the complexity of human knowledge has made specialization the rule, a theological student or young minister will often feel more sure that he possesses the knowledge and the skill for a specialized ministry, than that he shares the wider, more undefined gifts required for the parish pastor. The phenomenon of the specialized ministries, and the attraction they exert, should not be regarded as a *threat* to the churches, but they do constitute a *challenge*, a challenge to reflection and action at three distinct points.

1. In the first place, the specialized ministries challenge the churches *to take seriously their responsibility for their specialist ministers*. Some of these ministries were, indeed, initiated and may still be maintained by particular groups within the churches, but, in general, this is not so. It is the churches themselves, responding to the needs of society, that have set up military, hospital and prison chaplaincies, lay training institutes, social and industrial ministries, structures for religious education, publishing or broadcasting and the like. So also the decision to appoint ministers to administrative and co-ordinating posts and to theological professorships, follows inevitably from other decisions taken by the churches. These men were trained in theological colleges and faculties along with other ministers, they remain (or should remain) on the roll of ordained ministers; very often they come from the ranks of the parish ministry and may wish to return to it (though they may not always succeed). In many cases they are appointed by the churches and employed by them (sometimes more directly than are the parish pastors); they remain subject ecclesias-

tically to the law and discipline of the churches. The churches cannot and must not forget about them.

The European survey, however, revealed that in some churches, and notably in those of the Reformed family, specialist ministers were not necessarily accorded the same rights and duties as parish ministers. Constitutionally, indeed, all Reformed ministers have an equal say in church government, but specialist ministers (other than theological professors) do not have an automatic right to sit in courts of the church, or in some cases they may have the right to sit but not to vote. And even where, as in Lutheran or Anglican churches, no such legal problem arises, specialist ministers often feel that the church authorities, on the one hand, and their ministerial colleagues, on the other, take little trouble to understand the peculiar difficulties which they encounter, in what is often a very exposed situation. It is sufficient to name two of these difficulties to which different groups of specialists are subject: the problem of re-entering the parish ministry when a terminable appointment expires, and the problem of loneliness and spiritual uprootedness which is a real hazard in administrative and ecumenical posts.

2. In the second place, the specialized ministries challenge the churches *to rethink and restate their doctrine of the ministry.* In Anglican and in Reformed churches (though in quite different ways) official doctrinal formulations both in confessional documents and in services of ordination, must be strained to breaking point if they are properly to apply to specialist ministers. All of them assume a congregation, but the specialist in religious broadcasting or the church executive has no congregation, or none that is visible to him. All of them assume that the minister will be called on to discharge all of the classical ministerial functions: preaching, teaching, celebrating the sacraments, pastoral care and oversight and so on. But some specialist ministers never preach, or hardly ever, and many never have an occasion to celebrate the sacraments except when taking the place of a local pastor in an emergency. It is possible, indeed, to classify

specialized ministries in terms of the particular function which they most often fulfil, but this is rather artificial, and in any case tends to exclude the sacramental function.

A later chapter will consider the doctrinal question in greater detail. At the moment it is sufficient to point out that one more reason for looking at it again, is the anomalous position of the specialist minister. It is also interesting to note that at least one church, the Reformed Church of France, has recently altered its constitution specifically to include specialist ministers in the doctrinal definition of ministry.

3. In the third place, specialized ministries challenge the churches *to develop a strategy for the use and deployment of all their ministers.* It is not enough to evolve a coherent strategy for the specialists alone, since the most difficult point is to relate their work to that of their colleagues in the parish ministry. Further, it must be confessed that the specialized ministries, as such, do not form a coherent pattern. Their origins are too diverse and too haphazard. In military circles it is usual to work out the strategy first and to deploy the troops later. But here it is a case of trying to integrate a lot of independent operations into a common strategy, without any assurance that the whole front is covered, or that the best troops are deployed in the right places. In other words, the specialized ministries we have are not necessarily the ones we *need* for a coherent witness and for the adequate service of the society in which we live.

Specialists and General Practitioners

In the last chapter we noted that some of the historical forms of the 'alternative pattern' we were describing had an evangelistic or missionary emphasis. Is this a common characteristic which will help us see the relation of the specialists to the parish pastors? Can we talk of a *missionary pattern* of ministry parallel and complementary to the *pastoral pattern* of the parish ministry?

The evidence seems to be against it. The specialized ministries of today do not all, by any means, have a missionary intention. In the classification adopted in the survey, the sector described as concerned with 'Evangelism and Communication' is the weakest. Even allowing for faulty classification, it is clear that the 'Administrative' and 'Educational' sectors are much stronger, and that most, though not all, of the ministers in these sectors are involved in the secondary functions of training and administration which, in a complex society, have become necessary if the work of the parish ministry is to be carried on. It is quite natural that the churches have most readily seen the need for specialists working in these fields.

Another group of specialist ministers in the survey (some 27 per cent of the total number) are doing work with a pastoral emphasis, in the sector of 'Pastoral work among special groups'. Such work is of long standing, for there have always been certain segregated groups in society (soldiers, prisoners, hospital patients, seamen, the deaf and dumb, and, more recently, university students and migrant workers) which a parish ministry organized on a purely geographical basis could not reach. Such ministers are specialists, not because they do different things from the parish minister—by and large they do the same things—but because they are able to speak with particular groups of people and to understand their special problems. Their ministry normally includes the regular ministerial functions of preaching and teaching, of leading worship and celebrating the sacraments, of pastoral care and discipline. Without fear of disapprobation, they can form congregations or 'halfway' congregations (*Paragemeinden*) and do most of their work with them and through them.

But this is not a complete description of their work. Many such ministers (especially youth and student pastors) would reject the view that their sole, or even their primary, function was a pastoral one. They would see their ministry as missionary and would consider that they had opportunities, denied to or not often recognized by parish ministers, for an evangelistic and prophetic ministry as well as a pastoral one. They would consider that their work lay at the growing points of society, in a way that the work of the minister in the traditional rural or suburban parish no longer does (the minister in the inner city or in a new housing area is in a different case). They would consider their ministry as directed to all who with them stood at that particular frontier of society and not just to the faithful Christians there. Certainly one of their tasks is to form Christian congregations, but to form them for mission, rather than to cherish them.

In a sense this is to return to an older view of the pastoral ministry, the view which saw the parish minister as the one who, in a particular place, was responsible for making clear the Word of God to every man, and for interpreting that Word in terms of the pressures and structures of society. We have seen how, in great measure, this view has been replaced by another, in which the professional minister is the leader (or functionary) of a Christian congregation. This process was an inevitable result of social change. What some would say is that this remains the task of the Church, but a task which must now be fulfilled in a different way and at different points.

The growing points of society are no longer in the local community but elsewhere: in education, in industry, in government, in leisure-time activities, in scientific research, in medical and welfare work. In these and other places Christians are present. The role of the minister in such situations is not that of the chaplain, to offer spiritual succour or to bind up the wounds of the combatants, but rather that of the 'pioneer', of the theological interpreter or possibly just of the Christian brother who is in equal uncertainty but who is prepared to struggle and to pray. In some cases the churches have appointed specialist ministers with this role chiefly in mind—notably in the field of student and youth work and in industrial mission.

Our final answer, then, to the question whether specialist ministers can be said to have a common missionary role, is that this is their proper role though not their only one, nor is it exclusively theirs. We must add that, at present, only some of the categories of specialist ministers (and only some ministers in each category) see their task in this way.

It is their proper role but not their only one, since many of them will in fact be concerned primarily with educational, pastoral or administrative tasks. It is not their exclusive role, since nothing could be more unfortunate than a dichotomy such as has existed in the past between a settled pastoral ministry with no missionary zeal, and an itinerant or dispersed missionary ministry with no sense of pastoral responsibility. What is required is a new understanding of the ministry as a whole as *both* missionary and pastoral, and a realization that in contemporary society specialists are every bit as necessary as parish pastors.

This is not to advocate a reshaping of the ministry along similar lines to the medical profession with its division between 'specialists' and 'general practitioners'. Specialist ministers are not like medical specialists; their concern is not with one part of the soul—but with the whole man! A better medical analogy would rather be with the university doctor or army surgeon who has specialized in general medicine but has a particular interest and experience in the needs of a special group.

The true lesson, perhaps, from the medical field, is the urgent need to reshape the ministry, as the medical profession is being re-shaped, on the basis of *team-work*. The parish pastor with his own special skill and experience should be able to call on the complementary skills of other specialists. In some cases a parish or group of parishes would have specialist ministers as part of a team ministry; in others, the specialist ministers would be based, as at present, on larger areas but would be at the call of the parish ministry when required. In this way the gulf between pastors and specialists would be bridged, and their work integrated. This process is certainly assisted if some ministers pass, as at present, from a pastoral to a specialized ministry and back again in the course of their career.

3 · Team Ministry

The argument of the last chapter has led us to a conclusion very similar to that reached by the West European Working Group of the recent World Council of Churches' Study on 'The Missionary Structure of the Congregation'[1] which suggested, among other things, that the proper unit of church life in Western industrial society would be a larger parish corresponding to an administrative or municipal district, what sociologists call a 'human zone'. The Christian congregation would then consist of all the Christians living and working in that area. A whole series of varied and flexible structures could be developed to further the mission of that congregation. These structures would include small groups gathering regularly for worship and for the proclamation of the Word of God. But there would be other structures as well. If some such pattern developed—and there have already been experiments of this kind both in Europe and elsewhere—it is likely that a team of ministers would be necessary, some of whom would replace the pastors of the present nuclear parishes while others might well have specialist functions. A similar view is expressed in the report of the Working Group on the 'Shape of the Ministry' set up by the British Council of Churches.[2]

In recent years there have been a number of experiments in so-called 'team ministry', and there has been a great deal of discussion about it. The experiments, however, have been of different kinds. There has, for instance, been a renewed understanding of community life within the Protestant churches, as manifest in the Iona Community in Scotland, and the Community of Taizé in France. Iona had a marked influence on the first team ministry in the inner city,

34

the East Harlem Protestant Parish in New York;[3] and this was followed by other similar experiments such as the Notting Hill Group Ministry in London. Post-war initiatives in France and Germany of a somewhat different kind also played a part: such as the *équipes* (teams) of young people working in the French inter-church aid organization, CIMADE, and the industrial teams of the Gossner Mission in Mainz-Kastel and in East Germany.

At the same time, a rather different kind of team ministry has developed in the Roman Catholic Church in France, partly as a result of the traumatic experience of the worker-priest movement in the forties and early fifties. The *Mission de France*, an official instrument of the French episcopate for carrying out a missionary ministry in the dechristianized areas of France, both urban and rural, is on a much larger scale than any of the other experiments. It comprises some 360 priests in more than 80 *équipes* sent into a parish or group of parishes for a period of time at the request of the bishop, to use whatever means seem appropriate to further the mission of God—not just to keep church buildings open and to undertake a regular cycle of services. The team as a whole, under its leader, is responsible to the Mission for the work it does and the different members do not have separate responsibilities except as the team agrees. In most teams several of the priests are engaged in part-time secular work. The Mission has a national organization, a bulletin,[4] its own research team and a theological seminary (until recently at Pontigny and now in Paris) through which all its priests pass. The *équipe* or team is not regarded just as a convenient device for the efficient performance of a common task on the basis of a distribution of functions. Rather it is the key to the whole, providing the necessary spiritual fellowship and pastoral support for a costly and unprotected ministry. It is by mutual subordination of team-members to each other both in seminary and in the field that the whole dimension of service in Christian ministry is to be understood. A strategy adopted for the sake of mission has led to new insights about the nature of the ministry. It is no accident that reflection on the priesthood originally stimulated by

35

the *Mission de France* has borne fruit in certain sections of the *Vatican Decree on the Life and Ministry of Priests*.

This French movement has been one of the factors influencing the development of team and group ministries in the Church of England. In an official booklet published in 1965,[5] some fifty of these are listed. They are of very different kinds, but fall into two groups: *team* ministries which consist of several priests working together in a parish often with other lay specialists associated with them; and *group* ministries, where a group of neighbouring parishes (either in an inner-city situation or in a scattered rural area) have entered into voluntary association and work as one unit. In the first case the leader of the team is legally the incumbent and the other priests are his curates; in the other there may be no legal bond between the parishes but the beneficed clergy agree to work as a team and to recognize one of their number as a leader. Some of these teams and groups have received considerable publicity. The recent report of the Church Assembly Commission on the Deployment and Payment of the Clergy[6] has suggested ways in which the establishment of further team and group ministries might be facilitated. Similar patterns are being developed in the Free Churches, and, in certain cases, interdenominationally. There are also experiments along these lines in the Church of Scotland and in Germany.

In spite of their variety these experiments do suggest certain conclusions. First, and perhaps most important, they suggest a way of getting beyond the 'one-man' pattern so prevalent in Protestant churches, in which the minister is a *prima donna* with a chorus of laymen. The interaction of team-members makes possible a more complex undertaking or one too large and too demanding for one man's resources. Again, it overcomes the isolation and sense of frustration which many parish ministers feel. It may even be regarded as a way of renovating from within the parish system as a whole, retaining what is valuable and at the same time alleviating tensions and allowing more flexibility.

Further, it facilitates ecumenical co-operation. Mixed teams are possible; in many situations they seem essential. Urban teams like East Harlem or the Metropolitan Associates of Philadelphia; industrial missions like those in Durgapur, India, or Tema, Ghana; ministries in new towns like those in Livingston, Scotland, and Columbia, Maryland—all these and many others have been developed on an ecumenical basis. There is little hope, indeed, of developing a comprehensive strategy of ministry on a regional or national scale, unless it is based on ecumenical co-operation.[7]

Then, finally, as the *Mission de France* has found, team ministry has rediscovered a basic truth about the ministry which recent patterns of ministry, both Protestant and Catholic, have greatly neglected, its corporate or 'collegial' character. Membership of a team ministry is a source of spiritual strength to individual ministers, and may serve also as a nucleus for the growth of a Christian community.

This last point, however, leads to an aspect of team ministry requiring further study. The widest and most systematic use of teams to date has been in the Roman Catholic Church. Protestants tend to ask whether the concept of the team ministry, as a spiritual family and not merely as a practical device, is not too closely linked with the institution of a celibate clergy. Reformation teaching replaced the monastery by the family as the typical instance of a Christian community. The minister's family was supposed to be an example to other families, and in that sense the nucleus of the congregation. Of course the family has changed—nor was this ever an easy witness to maintain—but some would hold that to focus the congregation on a team of ministers would be a retrograde step. In any case, careful reflection is required on the minister's respective responsibilities to his family and to the team.

Another tricky point, which is closely related, is that of lay participation in the team itself. In the *Mission de France*, the team is a team of priests although a larger group of lay militants is often associated with it. Some of the Anglican teams have lay members: professional social workers, youth workers and others in the church's employ. This has, of course, been the traditional pattern in the foreign mission field. Many would welcome a development in this direction, holding that the theological and pastoral gifts of the minister must be complemented in the work of the Church by the professional competence of teachers, social workers, psychiatrists, sociologists and others. A conference at Gelnhausen, Germany, in 1966, which considered the problems of 'professional church-workers other than the clergy', was strongly in favour of this. They advocated a strategy in which the work at present done by ordained ministers, often isolated and ill-equipped for the task, would be done instead by a team of professionals, some lay, some ordained, having a variety of qualifications and working together with a wider group of voluntary or part-time specialists. This raises two problems which we must now go on to discuss: (1) What is the particular contribution that the ordained minister brings to a team of this kind? (2) Would such a team provide a valid modern equivalent to the New Testament description of a Christian community with diversified ministries and gifts?

The Minister's Professional Function

The question of the minister's role and function is usually expressed in professional terms. It is assumed that the minister is a professional man, and the ministry is a profession.[8] Every profession (as understood today) involves a particular expertise, a prolonged training, commitment to a norm of public service and accountability to certain professional standards and to a professional group. The ministry clearly possesses some of these characteristics, but what is its expertise, what is its function, what does a minister's training fit him to do? These questions are not easily answered, and this difficulty contributes not a little to the current malaise of ministers and theological students.

The function of the minister has not always been uncertain. In an earlier period, his role as spiritual leader of the local community was unchallenged. And more recently, in the nineteenth century for instance, the professional function of the minister could be seen as complementing those of other professional men: the doctor, the lawyer, and so on. The function of the minister in the community was the same as his function in the congregation; that of prophet, priest, and pastor—to proclaim the Word of God, to mediate wholeness and healing, and to care for the sick and needy. But today the community is not interested in God's Word, and the congregation is no longer prepared to receive it handed down from the pulpit. The community looks for wholeness and healing to other sources, to the psychiatrist for example, and the congregation is beginning to realize its own priestly role. The pastoral function in the community is eroded by the increase of the helping professions, and in the congregation it is beginning to be seen as a corporate task.

Various attempts have been made to discover the continuing function of the ministry by listing the different roles expected of the pastor in particular situations with a view to isolating the constant elements. But these roles are so varied, and the expectation of congregation and of community so often ill accords with what the pastor himself believes or has been taught, that no definite conclusion emerges.[9]

In the last two chapters we have stressed the diversity of situations in which ministers are at work today. In these situations different roles are expected of them; this complicates the task still further. One solution, of course, is to hold that the ministry as a profession is in process of being replaced by a whole group of distinct but related professions, sharing indeed a common commitment and certain elements of basic training, but with different professional functions.

But this is not a universal pattern; it cannot apply to those churches which have a real shortage of clergy. If the ministry of an African or Asian church is to be more diversified, touching men and society at more points than in the past, laymen must be ready to assume some of these roles and functions on a voluntary basis.

Patterns of Ministry

Though in certain exceptional cases it may be possible to build up teams of specialists with professional qualifications as in Europe or North America, this will probably be dependent on funds and personnel from abroad.[10] A team ministry of a different kind is, however, quite possible using the gifts, the education and the spare time that different laymen may have available. In such a team the role and function of the pastor may well vary, depending on his training and on his gifts. This is, perhaps, a much closer approximation to the situation described in the New Testament.

All Sorts of Service

There are two passages in the New Testament which are often quoted in relation to the diversified functions of the ministry. These passages are I Corinthians 12 and Ephesians 4. It is not my intention to give a detailed exegesis of either passage, but merely to say that New Testament scholars today are agreed in understanding them as referring to a pattern of ministry very different from that to which we have been accustomed in the Western Church during the last few centuries. Whether, as some would maintain, there were a number of different patterns of ministry coexisting in New Testament times in different parts of the Church, or whether the evidence is too scanty for us to be sure what happened, these passages suggest a degree of diversity and flexibility with which we have become unfamiliar. The following four comments would probably receive a wide measure of agreement, and can serve as a basis for our further discussion.

1. In both passages, *the starting-point is God's gift rather than man's need*. The apostle does not say: 'You need ministers of such-and-such a kind', but: 'God has given you ministers like this'. This point is important in relation to what we have said above. It is tempting to assume that the churches should first assess the needs to be met and the tasks to be done, and in the light of these should determine what ministries and ministers they require. In doing so, they may

40

overlook the resources which in fact they have. The insistence on certain traditional patterns of ministry has put a brake on the development of other patterns; the insistence on a certain kind of education has limited the candidates available; the restriction of ordination to the male sex has perhaps made the Church more monochrome than it need be; the reservation of most ministerial functions to the clergy has certainly frozen the resources provided by the laity. Now that our views are changing on all these points, we can see what we may have lost. We cannot be certain that God only calls those who would fit into traditional patterns of ministry. Nor is there any reason to suppose that God will always give the same gifts to his Church that he has given in the past. What seems to be happening in the Church today is that new gifts are being given which we do not yet know how to use, and they are being given sometimes to people the churches would never have chosen.

2. The list of gifts and of services in I Corinthians 12 as in Ephesians 4 contains items of different kinds. Whatever may be the exact significance of the order in each case, it appears that *some gifts are meant primarily for use within the Church, and others for use outside.* To use a distinction made first by a theologian from Formosa,[11] some of them are 'church-directed', and some 'world-directed'. In other words, it is not clear where the 'pastoral ministry' stops, and where the 'missionary ministry' begins. Hans-Ruedi Weber, in *The Militant Ministry*, has distinguished between the original task of the apostles to be 'pioneers' in an expanding missionary situation, and 'the additional task of strengthening the nascent church' which emerges as soon as such communities are founded, as here in Corinth and Ephesus. He goes on to say: 'In Western Christendom . . . too one-sided an emphasis has been laid on the pastoral and leadership functions at the expense of the distinctive functions exercised by the pioneers and missionaries of the Church'.[12]

3. *The 'services' listed are not precise functions, still less are they*

offices constitutionally established in the Church—they are gifts which different Christians have received. We must not think of the Apostle as one man, the Prophet as a second, and the Teacher as a third, and so on, although this is the way these passages have traditionally been understood, in terms of the institutional structure of the Church. It is not a professional list at all, neither a list of different professions, nor of different specialities within one profession. There is no basis here for demarcation disputes between ministerial colleagues with different assignments. Further there is, as Canon J. V. Taylor has said,[13] 'a carefree inconsistency and a splendid indifference towards what John Robinson calls the "clergy-line".'[14] We cannot say which gifts merited ordination, or were consequent upon it. It appears that all Christians received some kind of gift (Paul says so in so many words in I Cor. 12:7), but neither of these lists is meant to be exhaustive, they merely indicate some of the gifts that were given. In short, the ministry which is diversified, is not limited to the professional ministry.

4. *None of the gifts are given for the profit of those who possess them alone; they are given for the Church.* All these services are subordinated to the community as a whole, to 'Christ's body' of which each member is 'a limb or organ'. This points to a co-ordinated strategy in the Church as a whole, but it points more immediately to an intimate partnership within every Christian community. 'Team ministry' is not just a newly discovered device which may be a useful tool in certain contexts; rather it is something implied by all Christian ministry, since the service of God is service of the community of the faithful and such service is essentially mutual. This mutual service is a pre-condition of the harmonious functioning and continued growth of Christ's body, the Church.

From this, it is clear that we cannot have a theology of the ministry without a theology of the laity. The same passages of Scripture which throw doubt on our inherited patterns of ministry, provide a charter for the participation of all Christians in the ministry of

Christ. Here and wherever else in the New Testament the ministry is spoken of, it is the ministry of Christ which is meant, that ministry which is given to the whole Church and in which each Christian has a share. To lay down the rights and duties of ministers, and then, in relation to them, the rights and duties of the laity (often more of the second than of the first) is to distort New Testament teaching.

Some theologians would go further than this, and maintain that these and other passages from the New Testament expressly exclude any pattern of ministry which takes from the Church as a whole any functions whatever and entrusts them to a special group of people within the Church. Thus for the Mennonite scholar, J. H. Yoder,[15] the multiplicity of pattern and flexibility of structure here portrayed are binding on the Church. Alone of all religions, he says, New Testament Christianity rejects the postulate of the 'religious specialist' and replaces it by the concept of a 'shared ministry' which at an early stage was misunderstood and lost. This is an extreme position, and one which most churches would not share—though some churches do hold it, notably the Pentecostal movement which today, in some parts of the world, is growing faster than any other Christian group.

In a later chapter we shall consider the justification for the almost universal Christian practice of setting apart certain members of the Church for a special 'ordained' ministry. Here we must note the very clear evidence for a ministry 'shared' between different members of the Church, whom today we would distinguish as ministers and laymen. The biblical concept of team ministry is even more radical, it would appear, than some of the experiments which are being tried out today. More experiment is required and more theological reflection. For this reflection the concept of the ministry as a profession may not be particularly helpful. If, however, a team ministry is not to consist solely of laymen, if it is to contain some specialists with a theological training, we must find some alternative way of answering the question: what is the particular contribution of the minister to such a team?

4 · Ministers at Work

What is it that ministers do? Let us try to answer this question empirically. If we can find some common element in the wide diversity of patterns which we have discovered, this may tell us what the function of the ministry is. Previous empirical studies have tended to concentrate on the different roles of the parish minister in Europe or North America. These are diverse enough; but we have seen that they represent only a small part of the total diversity. In order to throw the net as wide as possible, to consider patterns of ministry in widely differing geographical areas and confessional traditions, and with different specialist functions we shall look at five examples of ministers at work. These examples are all taken from books or articles written by the ministers concerned, or by others with their permission. I shall present them briefly, in my own words and in the present tense, indicating in the notes the original sources.

1. Father George is the parish priest of a village of 750 souls in central Greece. On Sundays he celebrates the Divine Liturgy, starting with matins at 6.30 and ending around 9.30. The congregation, which most of the year is largely women and children, starts coming at 8.30. At Christmas and Easter the men of the village come, and about half the villagers communicate. The congregation is at its lowest during the harvest and in the winter. After Liturgy, Father George goes to the village coffee shop and talks with people there. At 3.00 p.m. he holds a catechism for the three top forms of the local elementary school. During the week he sings vespers each day, visits the sick, issues certificates of different kinds. This leaves him

ample time to eke out his salary by supervising the cultivation of his fields in his native village which is nearby. He has received a secondary education followed by two years at a major seminary which means that he is one of eight priests in the diocese, 10 per cent of the total number with sufficient theological knowledge to preach and conduct catechism classes.[1]

2. The Rev. Gerry Hutchinson is the minister of a six-point charge in the United Church of Canada, 50 miles from Edmonton. Since his manse is 8 miles from the nearest village, he has opened an office in a seed and fertilizer store in Telfordville where the store-keeper is one of his lay preachers. The office also houses an extension library from the University of Alberta and is the headquarters of the local telephone company of which Gerry Hutchinson is secretary. As it is on the extreme edge of the prairies, Telfordville has poor soil and its farmer population, whose grandfathers bought land there without having seen it, were impoverished and leaderless when he went there in 1949. Having studied agriculture, Hutchinson has been able to demonstrate new varieties of grain and fertilizer, with the aid of his junior boys' club, and some local farmers have taken them up. He also acts as chauffeur and projectionist for school films, and uses every possible means to weld together into a community the scattered settlements from different ethnic and religious groups. It has been difficult to find people to help conduct services—the distances are far too great for him to visit each settlement every Sunday. It is out of the question to run such a vast pastorate as a one-man show and lay leadership and opportunities for lay training have gradually spread; the same people have naturally been leaders in both church and community. In this situation, the mission of the Church, according to Gerry Hutchinson, is to serve the long-range needs of the community as well as to minister to the spiritual needs of individuals.[2]

3. The Rev. Josiah Magu, an Anglican priest, is associate industrial

advisor to the Christian Council of Kenya. His work lies on the south side of Mombasa Island, known as Kilindini (place of deep water), where there are eleven berths, two oil jetties and dockyards. Josiah covers the whole port about once a week, visiting a different section each day. There is often opportunity for talking and meeting workers without interfering with their work. Once a month he leads a discussion with the port police; and he also meets trainees in the Cargo Handling Training School, discussing questions of all kinds about the Church and industry and about the Christian Faith. The workers include Muslims, Hindus, Parsees and Sikhs, Protestants and Roman Catholics, Christians and atheists. When someone asks him what he is there for, Mr. Magu hands him a small card printed in English and Swahili, with two small pictures: one a church and one a factory. In the middle there is the sentence: 'The Church and Industry, a programme of the Christian Council of Kenya to help the Church listen, learn and serve modern industry, the trade unions and the people in them.' Under the factory it says: 'Industry: the single most important fact of the 20th century.'[3]

4. The Rev. Michio Imai is an ordained pastor of the Kyodan (United Church of Christ in Japan). A former businessman he entered the ministry after World War II. After serving for ten years in a city church and in a rural congregation he moved to Kakogawa city in a rapidly expanding industrial area, where he exercises an unusual ministry to truck-drivers. According to the police, some 55,000 truck-drivers pass through Kakogawa every 12 hours; unlike factory workers they are without rest or recreation facilities, and there is a high rate of accidents. 'Pop' Imai, as he is called, started a restaurant, which is run by his wife, but which is also an approved preaching-point of the Kyodan. Parking their trucks nearby, drivers come in for a bowl of rice or bean soup, a rest and a clean shirt. On Sundays Mr. Imai conducts a service of worship in the restaurant. A large restaurant, with parking and sleeping facilities, a laundry and conference room, is projected for the future, and local business com-

panies and societies are contributing funds for this, as well as churches in Japan and overseas.[4]

5. One of the authors of a recent Roman Catholic book entitled *Le Prêtre dans la Mission*[5] worked for a number of years among the *blousons noirs* in the eighteenth arrondissement of Paris. He was only very gradually accepted by these rough and independent young people for whom there is no place in bourgeois society or in a bourgeois church. He did not try to link them up with a church club or with the *Jeunesse Ouvrière Catholique*. They did not regard him as a priest or chaplain, but, with some reserve, as a companion sharing some of the same interests as themselves. He tells how on one occasion he went off with them on a camping expedition and how, in camp, without telling them what he was going to do, he celebrated Mass. Curiously they gathered round him, though some of them had never been inside a church. But they saw that he was serious about what he was doing, and he was able to turn to them and to say, paraphrasing John the Baptist: 'It is not me you are gathered round, but one who is greater than I, whose shoes I am not fit to polish.' In telling this story, he adds the comment that we must penetrate the natural communities of men so that they can understand themselves as Eucharistic communities. The role of the priest in mission is 'to be at the centre of a pagan community, and then slip aside behind Jesus Christ'.

Three Aspects of Ministry

Many more 'case-studies' of this kind could obviously be quoted, but these five are enough, and they are sufficiently varied, to make the point. The activities in which these men spend their day are highly diverse; no two time-tables would be alike. A classification in terms of traditional ministerial functions—preaching, preparing sermons, conducting worship, pastoral calls, administration, etc.— would reveal large discrepancies, and leave large areas of time unaccounted for. Yet it is often in the extra, 'unprofessional' tasks, which do not come under any of these headings, that the real work of the ministry is done. For Gerry Hutchinson it is in keeping the telephone accounts; in serving bowls of soup for Michio Imai; or discussing motor-bikes for the young French priest. To classify such activities as 'pastoral' or 'evangelistic' tells us nothing, though up to a point this is what they are, and they are often both at once. But it is in doing such things, and, more particularly, in doing them in a certain way, that a minister fulfils his function. It is in a working-day composed of such disparate activities, that the character of his ministry becomes apparent and his gifts are used for the equipping of the Church.

In saying that he fulfils his *function* as a minister, we are not using the word in quite the same sense as before when we looked for the minister's professional function, that which distinguished him from other professionals and could only be done properly or effectively by one with his qualifications. A professional function is related to training, knowledge and skill and to an institutional setting, but it has other more general aspects. Professor G. R. Dunstan has suggested that the three key concepts for the understanding of the professional man are 'knowledge', 'person', and 'relationship'. He illustrates this in the case of medicine as follows:

'I hope that the doctor to whom I may have to entrust a life— one of my family or my own—will be a doctor tout à fait: "a certain kind of person"; that is, a man formed into a doctor by the exercise upon him of the medical *knowledge* which he has acquired since he was at school and which he is acquiring still; by trained *capacities* derived from his teachers and from the daily exercise of his medical practice; and by his *relationships*, those with his colleagues in the profession among others'.[6]

In the case of the clergyman his knowledge is called theology. It includes a doctrine of God, of creation and of salvation, a theological understanding of Jesus, an understanding of the society or community called the Church, and 'certain, actual, existential relationships between God and man'. 'The primary function of the priest-hood,' he says, 'is to symbolize in various ways these doctrines and relationships, and to be the focus or nucleus of their embodiment in the local community of believers.'

It is this, he says, that makes the professional minister 'a *person* of a certain kind'; it is also the basis of his *relationships* to others (what he does, as opposed to what he knows and what he is), which are summed up for Dunstan in the phrase 'the pastoral task'. This task he is concerned to relate closely to the theology on which it is based and also to distinguish from the social and medical expertise of the other helping professions as 'not a "secular" service but only a service derived from and governed by the Servant of God'.

G. R. Dunstan is writing as an Anglican with the English social scene in mind. He is thinking primarily of the parish clergy and not of the specialists, nor of those somewhat unusual patterns of ministry described in this chapter. But I believe that he has put his finger on three general aspects of the minister's function which have a wider validity. Whatever the precise nature of a minister's particular duties or responsibilities, they can be understood in terms of what he knows, of what he is, and of what he does. What he knows is theology—not academic theology, but theology related to life in the world. What is important (as we shall see in the latter part of this book) is not a knowledge of facts, but a theological understanding of what God is doing in the world—a *theological awareness*. What he is is a Christian, but a Christian who represents the presence of the Church, the presence of Christ in a particular situation. His being there is a *Christian presence*. What he does is to *serve others*, in whatever way seems appropriate. Someone must do these things if the Church is to exist.

1. *Theological awareness* is a basic necessity. In Scotland as in Kenya, in Alberta as in Greece, someone is required who can see, and when occasion comes explain to others, what God has done and is doing in his world. The catechism class of Father George and the dockside

discussions in Mombasa are alike occasions when men and women can wrestle with the meaning of life and of history, with the issues of today and of tomorrow, and with the Word which God is speaking to his Church. The minister does not need to stand in the pulpit, or at the blackboard—it is probably better that he should not. Strictly speaking no professional minister is necessary at all, but without him, without someone trained to think in this way (ordained or lay, professional or amateur), the dialogue and reflection might not have taken place. This indeed is not so much an argument for a professional clergy, as for theological education—and for theological education of a new kind. But if there is a professional minister, he must be theologically aware, and he must keep his eyes open, too, for others who have this gift.

2. *Christian presence* is a popular phrase, but one often misunderstood, since it is thought to imply a silent but recognized presence which neither acts nor speaks. This is not what is intended. Presence is creative: it is a form of witness. The desire of the churches in Kenya to 'listen, learn and serve modern industry' is a case in point. The work of Josiah Magu symbolizes this desire, in the same way that the eucharist celebrated 'in camp' points to Christ's presence at the centre of a 'pagan community'. The minister, in Dunstan's words, is a 'focus or nucleus' of the doctrines of the Church embodied in the local community. The professional minister represents the Church, but he does not do so alone. It is the local community as a community which is the sign of Christ's presence, and of the presence of the Catholic Church. The minister, or any Christian, is there to stimulate, if he can, the creation of community, a community of which the true focus is not the Christian but Christ. Presence is not an alternative to preaching; it provides the context, the living link, within which alone preaching can be meaningful. The Christian who is present is seeking to create the conditions for dialogue. Presence is provocative, it requires a response. As such, it is the most effective form of evangelism.

3. *Service to others* is also essential. This aspect of ministry is most easily seen by the community at large. The ministry to truck-drivers in Japan is a different kind of service from that of community development in the prairies. Hutchinson is no more a professional agriculturalist than Imai is a welfare worker. Both of them, in a sense, are acting outside their professional fields; but there is no one in either situation whose professional responsibility it is to perform these particular services, and therefore the Church must perform them. Service of others is binding on all Christians. Those who bear the title of 'minister' dare not forget that all ministry is derived from the ministry of Christ who took upon himself 'the form of a servant'. There is an ambiguity, indeed, in this description, since it is not always clear whom the minister should serve: God or the people. 'It is the essence of the Christian concept of ministry to affirm both . . . and to hold the two in dynamic tension. Ideally, the minister is at one and the same time a servant of God and a servant of the people. He fulfills his service to God by helping people in need, and he best serves the people by remaining faithful to the sovereign God.'[7]

Professionals and Non-Professionals

Ministry as we have described it is not the preserve of the clerical profession. In this chapter we have argued empirically from what ministers actually do, and we have been able to discover certain essential elements in the function of the ministry. They do not, however, help us to distinguish ministers from laymen, since all Christians are called—according to their gifts—to theological awareness, Christian presence and service to others. How can a minister be thought of as a professional, if his function is merely to do what all Christians must do?

In the next chapter we must ask the theological question about the meaning of ordination. We shall conclude this one by considering the changes going on in the whole concept of the profession, as described by the German sociologist and theologian, Justus Freytag, in a paper entitled 'The Ministry as a Profession'. In Western society, today, three things are happening, Freytag says:

a 'for the man of today his professional occupation forms only a fractional area alongside other areas of life. His profession does not absorb the whole meaning of his life or the whole of his day.'

b 'The process whereby activities determinative for the whole of life are split up into individual professions has already reached the stage in modern society at which it is thought that all important work must take on the guise of a profession . . . The part-time or honorary position in the political community, in societies and associations is disappearing.'

c 'The man of today is compelled to orientate himself so exclusively according to the pattern of professional activity because his profession forms the decisive line between the individual and society as a whole. . . . Concern for social security and the linking of profession and social prestige oblige men in the society of today to seek affirmation of their existence in objectively defined achievement and in professional advancement.'[8]

The professional minister is in a particularly awkward situation. Unlike other professionals his professional role and his role in private life are inseparably related. In order to demonstrate his professional competence he is forced either to concentrate on building up the Church as an organization or on claiming to represent the Church as an institution in the larger community. Both ways, however, entail unforeseen consequences, since, in the first case, the minister will find himself 'contributing with his authority to the development of the congregation as a distinct group within the district', and, in the second, by giving 'expert supervision to ensuring the correctness of church life, . . . he involuntarily collaborates in the petrification of ecclesiastical forms and in the detachment of the Church from the centres of social life.'

Taking these changes into account, and the decline, mentioned above, of the part-time involvement of professional people in private associations—including the Church—a new understanding of the ministry becomes essential. The solution is not to be found, according to Freytag, by distinguishing the function of the minister and the layman, by maintaining that 'the function of the minister . . . is to equip the lay person for service and for encounter in his professional daily life.' It is important to stress that neither for ministers nor for laymen today is a man's profession to be taken as the chief or only place of his Christian calling and obedience—as was the case at the time of the Reformation. In fact, 'the minister finds himself in the same situation as the lay person'; he must make it clear 'that Christian witness is not exhausted in the fulfilment of limited professional services.'

Freytag suggests two practical ways of doing this which by no means exclude each other: (1) the minister can play his part in other roles in the political and public sphere outside his professional activities; and (2) the Church might 'confer full ministry also on members of the congregation who are engaged in other professions'. This would show that a minister's function is not defined by the particular tasks he performs. It would also demonstrate that the calling of the minister is no different from that of 'every Christian in his secular profession or occupation'.

This last suggestion has been widely discussed ecumenically since the publication in 1965 of a booklet entitled *A Tent-making Ministry* which outlined the scriptural and historical precedents for ministers in the Church who, instead of recurring a stipend from their congregation or out of church funds, earned their own living by the work of their hands, as did Paul by making tents. It also enumerated certain experiments conducted in Asia notably by the Anglican Church in Hong Kong and by the Diocese of Madurai in the Church of South India. In both cases the principal justification for the step was the shortage of professional ministers and the impossibility of their ministering adequately to the needs of a scattered and growing church. Once the step had been taken, other

53

advantages appeared. In Hong Kong, for instance, the auxiliary clergy were of a higher educational level than the 'professionals', since by profession they were mostly teachers, civil servants or engineers. The church was enabled in this way to have the service and leadership of mature men with a widespread knowledge of the world, who would not otherwise have formed part of the church's ministry. In South India, on the other hand, the situation is somewhat different. Here the advantage seemed to be that the natural leaders of a village community were ordained as ministers without being separated from the community by social, economic or educational gulfs. Problems, of course, exist, but it is safe to say that many churches in Africa and Asia are attracted to this solution of a perennial difficulty and are anxious to learn from the experience of such 'tent-making' schemes.[9]

A different kind of 'tent-making ministry' has been attempted in the Roman Catholic Church, especially in France. The 'worker-priest movement' of the forties and fifties attracted a great deal of attention outside France, especially because of its later discontinuance. Many churches, and especially Anglican churches, became convinced of the validity of what the worker-priests were trying to do, though uncertain how it would apply in their own situation. There has been much discussion in the Anglican church of the desirability of 'part-time priests', and certain priests both in England and Canada have, on their own initiative, though with the sanction of their bishops, taken work in factories or elsewhere instead of, or in addition to, ecclesiastical appointments.[10] Developments in France since 1954 have been less publicized, but are of the greatest significance. Although till recently forbidden to work full-time in factories, many priests, both of the Mission of France and of religious orders, have engaged in part-time manual work and in doing so have found themselves liberated from the constraint of their professional role in church and in society. At the same time, they have found it easier to enter into dialogue with those, both workers and intellectuals, who are alienated from the Church.

In 1965, the French episcopate sanctioned a new initiative of *prêtres au travail* to engage full-time in secular work, and the *Decree on the Life and Ministry of Priests* explicitly refers to the possibility of priests sharing by manual labour 'in the lot of the workers them-selves—if there seems to be need for this and competent authority approves'.[11]

These experiments merit further study and it is hoped that in the next few years a critical analysis can be undertaken of what has happened with an attempt to draw on their theological implications.[12] A number of churches are very greatly interested in the possibility of supplementing their professional ministry by a certain number of ministers who would in fact belong to other professions. It must, however, be remembered, as Bishop Lesslie Newbigin indicates in his Preface to *New Forms of Ministry*, that 'the question is not, "What special and exceptional arrangements must we make in order to keep the traditional pattern of the ministry from breaking under the new strains?". The question is, "What in the new circumstances into which God has thrust us, is the pattern of ministry which is proper to the nature of the Church as God's apostolic community in this world?" '[13]

That pattern may not basically be a professional pattern. Indeed, if Freytag is right, to speak of the ministry as 'a profession' or of ministers as 'professionals' may always be to speak with a certain irony. The ministry cannot be considered as a profession like others; it is always more than a profession, and its very existence is a threat to the other professions. However desirable it may be that ministers should be more 'professional' than they are (in Scherer's sense) as regards their objectivity, attitudes, ethics and training, the line distinguishing them from 'laymen' cannot be hard-and-fast.

5 · Why Ordination ?

In the Montreal Report, David M. Paton refers to the fact that the ecumenical discussion on the ministry has changed its character in the last twenty-five years. This results from two things: the recovery of the doctrine of the whole Church as the people of God, and the recovery of 'a sense that the Church, the ministry, and the congregation are all alike in basic principle missionary, though much of the structure we have inherited from the past makes it difficult to practise this principle and to act upon it.'[1]

These factors have hardly begun to influence, however, the official formulations of the churches of the doctrine of the ministry, in their confessional and constitutional documents and their ordination services. This fact became apparent when, as part of the survey of specialist ministers in Europe, described in Chapter 2, the European churches were asked for copies of such official statements. In most cases the statements in question were based on sixteenth-century originals; changes made in recent centuries were mainly changes in wording, and in any case still assumed a pattern of church life where professional pastors are responsible for discharging, more or less unaided, a preaching, pastoral and liturgical ministry. In these documents there is no suggestion that the whole congregation shares in the ministry of Christ, or that individual Christians have received gifts of ministry which must be given expression in the Church.

Certainly a number of churches are beginning to see the need to reformulate their official statements; although those reformulations so far adopted have been extremely cautious. It is encouraging, however, to note that a number of the church commissions currently engaged in this task are going back to first principles, and are trying to find ways of restating what they believe in terms which take account of our rediscovery of the laity and of the mission of the whole people of God. At this point we might well take a lesson from the Roman Catholic Church, which by the *Vatican Decree on the Life and Ministry of Priests*, has shown readiness to adopt officially a markedly different view of the ministry from that which was previously current. It is noteworthy, too, that in the *New Catechism* published by the Roman Catholic bishops in the Netherlands, the treatment of 'the Pastoral Priesthood' is preceded by a chapter on 'the Priesthood of the People of God', and begins with a paragraph on 'Service'.

In view of this, we must welcome the current study on Ordination of the Faith and Order Commission of the World Council of Churches. A first working-paper has already been produced by a small consultation at Geneva in April 1968.[2] It suggests some fruitful lines of ecumenical study and directs some searching questions to those churches which are presently considering the subject.

It is not my intention, in this chapter, to pursue this discussion further but merely to draw attention to two views on ordination which cut across confessional lines and which are closely related to developments in patterns of ministry. One of these arises directly from experience and frustration in the practice of the ministry. The other is based on theological reflection on the ministry of the laity and on the mission of the Church.

The Radical Position

The question 'Why Ordination?' is being asked pointedly by an increasing number of theological students, laymen, and younger ministers all over the world. For them the precise function of the ordained minister has become so vague, the traditional teaching on the subject so inappropriate, that they despair of receiving an intelligible answer. For many of them this is the Christian doctrine which requires the most to be demythologized. When they try to explain to their contemporaries what the churches believe about the ministry, they are well aware that their explanation sounds like magic. In discussions in Europe, North America and Asia, with younger ministers and active laymen, and with their seniors as well, time and again the view is expressed that the concept of *ordination* is no longer helpful in understanding the Church's ministry and in planning its work. They are not on the whole inclined to dismiss the need for professional ministers; those who are ministers themselves are well aware that they have things to do which are important and would not otherwise get done, but they do not see why a man or a woman need be ordained to do them. If 'ordination' is merely the technical term for licensing a professional clergyman, they would say, well and good; authorization of this kind is essential—but let it be for a limited period. If it is merely equivalent to the award of a theological degree, that also is comprehensible; we need theologians—though not too many of them, and only in certain jobs. But if it means, as the churches have hitherto taught, the conferring of a different status and a permanent function on a select group within the Church, it is both unnecessary and undesirable. In any case, the mystique surrounding it should be done away with.

This feeling of exasperation with what the churches apparently teach, accounts for the widespread popularity of a view of the ministry based on the assertion that 'baptism is the ordination of the laity'. This thesis stems from the ecumenical study on baptism conducted by the Faith and Order Commission before the New Delhi Assembly[3] and was later seen to have considerable implications for the discussion on the ministry. In a document prepared for the Montreal Conference, the World Council of Churches' Department of Laity commented:

'This ordination of baptism is basic for the whole study of the ministry. One may understand and interpret any subsequent special ordination within the Church quite differently, but this basic once

and for all life-long ordination of baptism remains valid. Every
specially ordained minister in the Church is and remains first of all
a baptised member of the Church'.[4]

Although this statement explicitly states that different 'under-
standings' and 'interpretations' of ordination are possible, much
subsequent discussion has assumed that this is all that need be said,
or indeed can be said, about ordination. Put bluntly, if all Christians
are ordained, a second ordination makes no sense; all that matters
is that different Christians should be enabled and authorized to
carry out such functions as are necessary for the good of the church
according to the gifts they have received. Professional ministers may
well be required, but even they should receive no further ordination.

This point of view quite naturally appealed to many of those
involved in the Study on 'the Missionary Structure of the Congregation', since it appeared to give the necessary theological basis
for a strategy such as we have outlined at the beginning of Chapter 2.
It had the further advantage of removing any source of friction
between the 'lay' specialists and the 'ordained', since on this view
all are ordained and have received training and authorization from
the church for different but complementary ministries. The
'ordained minister' or 'theologian' is only one member of a team of
ministers belonging to different professions and with different gifts.
His function as a member of the team is to help in equipping the
others for their work.

A telling illustration of what this might imply may be seen in the
description of the 'service-teams' of the Gossner Mission in the
German Democratic Republic which went to work in the new
industrial towns where there is no legal provision to appoint a
pastor or to establish a new parish. The teams, consisting of young
people, some of them theological students but none of them
ordained, earned their living by working in factories. After some
time, they succeeded in forming larger groups which included
Christians from other parts of Germany, together with workers

who, though they would not call themselves Christians, were deeply concerned that in this impersonal milieu no real community existed. As the 'congregation' grew larger, and 'pastoral' needs multiplied, the team nominated a different member in turn to act as 'pastor' for a month, working half-time and supported by the earnings of the others. At the same time, they petitioned the church authorities for ordination, so that the sacramental functions of the ministry could also be carried out. Not wishing to introduce a distinction between team-members which did not correspond to the ministry they performed, they asked for ordination to be conferred not on one of the theologians of their number, but instead on the whole group.[5]

Ministers as Pioneers

A full acceptance of the ministry of the laity does not, however, commit us to rejecting ordination. Indeed, it can be argued that if all Christians are faithfully and effectively to fulfil their ministry, then it is necessary for some to be set apart for the specific purpose of seeing that the whole Church does its job. It is this 'enabling' function which is part of the meaning of ordination.

Thus, Hans-Ruedi Weber, in *The Militant Ministry*[6] refers to the need for special troops to support a fighting army. 'The militant church', he says, 'needs soldiers who are set apart for the work of pioneering, for services of communication . . . for training and for oversight.' All Christians are called to participate in the apostolic mission to the world. But there is need also for 'an apostolic *mission to the church*'—and it is this that is carried on by the ordained ministry. This 'includes at least the following three functions: (a) the function of pioneering in and for the church, (b) the function of strengthening the church in its life and mission and (c) the function of uniting the church for its task in the world.'

Weber does not reject the position that 'baptism is the ordination of the laity'. But he does not reject either the need for further ordination within the ordained laity. The above thesis is *part* of what the churches have meant by baptism; but it is not *all* they have meant by ordination. Commitment to a particular ministry within the people of God should represent a further step of obedience beyond the general commitment to follow Christ.

But the function of ordained ministers is not just to equip laymen for their task—what Weber refers to as 'the service of the army cook'. As a member of the militant people of God, the 'set-apart' minister must share in the actual fighting, in the apostolic mission with which God's people is entrusted. Nor indeed can ministers adequately equip others for a battle in which they themselves have no part. And so, for Weber, the concept of the 'equipper' must be completed by that of the 'pioneer'.

The Pioneer Ministry is the title of a book by Anthony Hanson, who reformulated his doctrine of the ministry when working as missionary in South India after the Church of South India had been formed. During this experience he came to see that the fullness of the ministry was present in other confessions than his own. Returning to Scripture, he sought for a doctrine of the ministry in the biblical writings as a whole. He discovered the clue in the Old Testament conception of the Remnant and in Paul's references in the Epistles to his own work and that of his colleagues. According to his view, no clear distinction is made in the New Testament between 'the ministry' on the one hand, and 'the Church' on the other, simply because the one merges into the other.

'The ministry is originally the Church *in nucleo*, the faithful Remnant whose task is to gather others and lead them also in carrying the Ministry of the Messiah . . . The Apostles were not something else plus the Church or over the Church. They were the first Church, and hence the Church is apostolic in as far as it carries out the task which the apostolic Remnant carried out, proclaims the redemptive acts of God in history, witnesses to the prophecy fulfilled, lives out the self-emptying ministry of Christ in the world . . . The ministry is the apostolic mission of the Church: its task is essentially pioneer, it is the spearhead of the Church'.[7]

Professor Hanson suggests that there are many different patterns of ministry which might correspond with the biblical insight he has exposed. He endorses, for instance, a greater extension of the tent-making ministry.[8] The ordained ministry is essential, but not all ministers need to be professionals. Further, it is not their professional functions which make them ministers, but their representative and pioneer character in the Church. The clergy is not 'a special group or corporation marked out by the fact that they are permitted or empowered to perform certain actions which laity are not permitted to perform'. Rather the distinction is between those who lead in certain actions, and those who are led. 'But the actions are not the actions of the clergy, but of the Church'.[9]

Weber and Hanson are chiefly concerned to develop a theology of the ministry which fits in with our new ecumenical insights. Other theologians, taking much the same position, have tried to develop a pattern of ministry which would reconcile the function of ministers and of laymen. Among these, we may cite the Bishop of Woolwich, who, in his Prism Pamphlet *Meeting, Membership and Ministry*[10] maintains that ordination, baptism and confirmation have all been administered in terms of a situation which no longer obtains in which the world is seen as inside the Church, and in which 'ministry is the prerogative of the élite'.

In the new situation of today, he suggests that the relationship of *Meeting* (an attitude of response and attention) should be taken as normative for all who are not yet ready to take the definite step of Church membership, including the children of church members. *Membership*, which would be marked by baptism administered to adolescents, would be understood as incorporation into the Body of Christ and would include communicant status. The third stage, which he calls *Ministry*, would be for those who were ready to take their Christian calling seriously in terms of commitment to mission and service. It would be marked by a rite equivalent to confirmation. All so 'ordained' would be equally ministers, whether or not they later underwent training for specialist ministries in addition to their secular trade or profession. Some of these ministries would be purely functional and temporary.

The Scandal of Ordination

The different views of ordination listed in this chapter have this in common, that they all take seriously the ministry of the laity and the mission of the Church. In this, they are distinguished from more traditional views of ordination, and they are far easier to reconcile with each other, in spite of their differences. There may not even, in the last resort, be a basic division between those who reject the concept of an ordination subsequent to baptism and those who maintain its validity and significance.

To my mind, indeed, the latter position is more agreeable to Scripture, than the alternative one which rejects ordination as meaningless today. It also takes far more seriously what the churches have, in the past, tried to say about ordination. I do not think that an ecumenical theology can afford to ignore the traditions of the churches even when they appear to be wrong; and in this matter it seems to be important to discover the unchanging truth in what is said, even though the ways in which it has been said now seem unacceptable.

Those who reject the concept of ordination as out of date and mythological are forgetting an important biblical truth, that ministry, of whatever kind, always implies selection. The Bible constantly witnesses to the fact that particular men and women are called by God to serve Him in a way which sets them apart from others who are not so called. This was true of the patriarchs and the prophets in the Old Testament, and also of those who bore the office of king and priest. It is true also of Israel as a people among the nations. It was eminently true of Christ, and after him, of the apostles, but not only of the apostles. It is indeed true of the Church as a whole and of all Christians both in the first centuries and today.

If the doctrine of election is seen as a scandal, then ordination is also a scandal, since it implies that some people are needed for special duties, the precise nature of which is not clearly defined. As Robert S. Paul has suggested,[11] ordination can be seen as the Church's acknowledgement that God is setting apart a particular person for his own purpose, together with the Church's acceptance of that person as an instrument through whom God chooses to work. The fact that some men and women are set apart by the Church's act in response to God's call is a needful reminder of where the Church's obedience lies; while the witness and service of those set apart is both the first-fruits of the Church's obedience and, at the same time, helps make that obedience possible.

But the obedience of Christ and of his Church is an obedience in suffering. A further element in the 'scandal' of ordination arises from this. Christ has given the Church 'ministers to be its forerunners and helpers in its sacrificial life'.[12] This point is well put in the final chapter of *The Militant Ministry*.

It is imaginatively illustrated, too, in that remarkable parable of the Church and the ministry, *God in my Unbelief*, by J. W. Stevenson,[13] where the young minister whose story it tells reflects as follows on the failures of his first year in a Scottish country parish: 'The minister was to be no mere offerer of a sacrifice for his people. He was himself to be a sacrifice, himself an offering, a faith for them before God, so that their faith might be kindled. The need of the Cross, his need of the Cross must be visible before them.' And, in another place: 'This is our calling—to go out with decisive steps even while we are in hesitancy, to go to the act of thanksgiving before we know we are healed, to distribute Christ's bread to the hungry before we know it will be sufficient. It is not for us to know certainty but to learn to trust ourselves to God, and to do what we know He is expecting of us while we are still uncertain.'

The final sentence leads to another comment. Many ministers today, perhaps more then ever before, are seeking for a meaning in their ministry, aware that to human weaknesses and the limitations of ecclesiastical and social structures, there is added theological uncertainty which strikes more deeply at them than at those who are theologically unschooled. Perhaps it is not for them to know certainty, or for the churches either as they seek to reformulate their traditional views of the ministry. It may be part of God's purpose that the question of ordination should remain for the time unresolved. We may only be able to understand clearly the purpose of the ministry in the Church, when the churches have committed themselves more fully to reunion and renewal.

Part Two

Theological Education

6 · What is Theological Education?

'What is Theological Education? Should it be mainly concerned with the preparation of full-time ministers or priests serving a local congregation? Or has the time come to conceive theological education in a much broader way as the education of leaders who may express their Christian vocation in many different ways and not necessarily as full-time church workers?'

The Advisory Group appointed by the World Council of Churches in 1967 to review the work of the Theological Education Fund asked this question of more than a hundred persons involved in theological education throughout the world. The answers received almost invariably described a function wider than that of training a professional ministry. 'Theological education seems to be concerned', wrote one respondent, '(a) with the task of research and reflection concerning the mission of the Church today, (b) with the preparation for witness of all members of the Body.' Another summarized his reply in the brief phrase: 'to enable the people of God to share in the mission of Jesus Christ to all men.' The other answers were in a similar vein, many of them going on specifically to refer to the education of the laity, in addition to and often alongside the education of a professional ministry.

Theological Education viewed as a Whole

This emphasis on the theological education of the whole people of God is a constant refrain in recent ecumenical discussion. It figures in the reports of consultations held in Asia, Europe, North America and the Pacific between 1964 and 1968,[1] as also in studies done in Africa and Latin America. It was, as we shall see, a major emphasis

69

of the Northwood Consultation held in July 1967. It is stressed in the reports of commissions established by individual churches, and it appears, time and again, in books and articles written on the subject. The argument no longer starts with the need for a professional ministry and leads on to the precise requirement of theological education. Rather it starts from the existence of the Church, or from the character of theology itself and goes straight to the theological education of the laity (the ministry being simply considered as a special group with special needs).

One leading Asian theologian goes further, and considers the Church as 'at best a secondary determinant' of theological education. 'The primary determinants', he writes, 'are God and the world. Theological education is a process through which a person learns to be human through what God has been and done in Christ', and so should not be confined to high-school or college graduates preparing for a professional, ordained ministry. Rather it should recruit for training committed Christians engaged in different professions and teach them to exercise their Christian faith in diversified ministries, in and through their professions. 'Lay-training should not be treated as a step-child of theological education. It has to be given a legitimate and equal place in what is going on ... What I would like to see happen', he concludes, 'is not the so-called laity taking over the function of the clergy more and more, but all Christians taking part in the mission of God in the world on an equal basis but in different ways.'[2]

These quotations are in accord with the view of ministry expressed in the first part of this book, but they may seem to be irrelevant to theological education as it is actually being conducted today. In fact, this is not so. Theological education has been changing, just as patterns of ministry have been changing, and neither change has been fully acknowledged by the churches. The New Delhi Assembly in setting up the study on theological education, from which this book comes, used as an equivalent term the phrase, 'training for the ministry'. Theological education today is already much more than this.

In the 400 theological schools in Asia, Africa and Latin America on the lists of the Theological Education Fund, 33 per cent of the students have no intention at the time they enter of proceeding to the professional ministry; 56 per cent of the schools are carrying on some form of theological education for the laity.

Again, in North America, the recent increase in number and popularity of Departments of Religion in state universities and in private colleges has changed the situation radically.[3] The distinction between the 'study of religion' carried on in these schools and the 'theological education' of the seminaries is becoming more and more artificial. There is a growing desire among students today to study Christian theology at the university level without vocational commitment. Coupled with this, few among the students entering theological schools (and the total enrolment of North American seminaries was higher in 1968/69 than in any previous year) have reached the maturity in Christian faith and clarity of vocational commitment that was normal in earlier years. As the head of one school has put it, 'the trend is for fewer and fewer men to come with clarity of conviction about the Gospel and the Church and their place in them. . . . More and more come to search . . . They come as enquirers. They ask questions . . . It is not knowledge that is sought so much as meaning'. Laymen and future ministers are basically looking for the same thing.

The Northwood Consultation on Theological Education, the final meeting of the series arranged by the World Council of Churches study, began its report by insisting that theological education is a *whole*, and that the education of the professional clergy is only one part of it. Within this whole, three different strands can be distinguished, all three of which traverse the full breadth of the fabric. The three strands they describe as follows:

a the pursuit of truth in open enquiry,
b the apprehension of the meaning of the Gospel as experienced in the confessing community, and
c vocational training for leadership roles.

Not every theological institution, of course, provides all three of these strands, but a complete theological education should provide them all.

Further, this should be as true of theological education for the laity as for the theological education of the professional ministry. 'The committed Christian who is *not* ordained expects, and is right to expect, from any course of theological education the same elements that are required in ministerial training. (1) He should be taught to pursue rigorously the question of truth. (2) He is right to expect theology to be related to the mission and life of the Church as well as to contemporary society; and he will hope to receive some spiritual formation by participation in a committed community. (3) He is also right to expect that he should be equipped for any ministry to which he is called.'[4]

This statement has certain clear implications which are not here spelt out fully though they are referred to in *Recommendation* 1, which asserts (a) that 'the planning of courses of theological education for ministers and laity should be related and co-ordinated as far as possible'; and (b) that 'shared courses should be the rule, where there is a comparable level of educational capacity'. A more far-reaching implication, though one which must be faced, is (c) that a 'theological education for the whole people of God' if planned and carried out as a whole would look very different from existing courses for ministers, on the one hand, and for laity, on the other, even when these are related to each other and are carefully co-ordinated. In the last chapter of this book, we shall look at this question further. Although it hardly formed part of the present study, it represents, in the view of many, the next stage of the ecumenical discussion on theological education.

Theology in a New Situation

What are the reasons which led the members of the Northwood Consultation, like the other witnesses quoted above, to this wider view of theological education? Most of them are engaged in theological education as traditionally understood. They are not speaking as radical theologians, nor as the leaders of lay academies, but as theological educators, for whom this wider view must imply considerable changes in what they are doing. They did not come lightly to the conclusion that the aims of the institutions in which they were teaching were now largely out-of-date. It was because of a firm conviction that the situation has changed, that they maintained, as they did, that theological education must now be understood as the theological equipment of the whole people of God.

What has changed is, primarily, the character and situation of theology. Whereas, in earlier days, theology was seen as a coherent system of belief which must be communicated to students and accepted by them intellectually in order to become the basis and motive force of their life and ministry, today it is being thought of in different terms. It is no longer regarded as a complete and established body of knowledge. Rather it may be thought of as a process of *exploration*. Theologians, in Kenneth Grayston's image, are like explorers travelling in unfamiliar country, seeking to understand the unknown in terms of what they know. Their method of proceeding and the equipment which they use are indeed supplied by their faith in God's action in Christ, but only because they believe that this 'corresponds to what is there in the stuff of human existence, and is more adequate than other tools for exploring the depth of that existence . . . The territory they explore is not decided by their faith and their discoveries are real discoveries'.[5]

The emphasis must be laid not so much on thinking as on *doing theology*. Theology is an activity in which all Christians are necessarily engaged (though they are not always aware of it). This point is strongly made in a report of a Church of England committee on theological education, discussed in Chapter 8. It has been expressed recently in a paper read by Professor Arnold B. Come of San Francisco to a consultation in India on the theological education of the laity. 'Theology', he says, 'is a living, moving, dynamic process that is never given to us by someone else either from the past or in the present ... Rather it is something that we do. We can possess theology and be theologically educated only by participating in the event that produces theology'.

How can we learn to do theology? The answer is not in doubt: by seeking to live as Christians in the contemporary world, applying our minds and our faith to the problems on 'the world's agenda'. As Richard Shaull of Princeton puts it, 'If theology today is to make sense, it must be forged in a constant running conversation between the tradition of faith—our biblical and theological heritage—and the contemporary situation'.[6] And Daniel Day Williams of Union Theological Seminary writes: 'The questions which are asked within the academic setting must be the questions, or related to the questions, which arise out of participation in the struggle for social justice, ministry to personal disorganization, and institutional reform. The present move for student power in the seminary must be viewed as part of the questioning of the theology of power taught in the seminary. For example, discussion of love of neighbour takes on a new aspect when the meaning of Christian community and educational institutions so long dominated by white interests, programmes, and instruction is raised by black students conscious of a new identity'.[7]

In an essay on 'Theological Education in a Revolutionary Society' Hiber Conteris of Uruguay makes the same point in a Latin American context. How can theological education adapt itself, he asks, to the new situation of the Church in a period of rapid social change? He answers, there are 'two concrete possibilities for a new goal for theological studies.' 1 They can supplement a liberal professional education. 'The student of theology might receive a university education and a professional training in the public system. His subsequent theological studies would have the limited aim of developing his biblical and doctrinal understanding of secular society. Such a student would go into a secular profession but would exercise a "tent-making ministry".' 2 But 'a theological vocation *per se*' is also conceivable, which would require a new kind of theological curriculum. Such a 'full-time theologian' would not be responsible for the administration of a local congregation but 'in the revolutionary society of Latin America, would exercise an activity in the field of theology comparable to that performed by a research-worker in the field of the social and natural sciences'. The function of the theologian, he concludes, is analogous to that of the interpreter, the key man, in our international organizations. 'God is speaking all the time, and a simultaneous translation is required.' Furthermore, the theologian must interpret in the other direction too, interpreting 'the confused murmurings of men'. 'His mission is to stand in the very centre of contemporary ideological currents, which represent secular attempts to understand history and society, he must give form to these attempts—which are always vague, frustrated, destined always to get lost and to be renewed in the incessant flux of history—in order to make them intelligible before God our grand interlocutor. It is in this that the greatness and the misery of theology always consisted, and still consist today.'[8]

In discussing theological education as it is today and the possible changes which can be made we must take account of the nature of theology and the situation of the Church in the world today. The place of theology is at the 'creative centre' of human culture.[9] Its task is to explore and to reflect on the depths of human existence, the goals of human society, contemporary ideologies and their attempts to understand the meaning of history. Such exploration and reflection demands an existential commitment to God's action in Christ; it demands also an existential involvement in the questionings and revolutions of men.

Our new understanding of theology has certain clear implications for theological education. It is *ecumenical;* theological education must therefore be in an ecumenical context. It is *for laymen* as well as for ministers. There is a strong case therefore for their studying theology together. It is *in dialogue* with human thought and culture; for many this would imply that the proper locus of theological study

75

is the university. It *requires actions* as well as words; theological education should therefore also include practical involvement in the activities of the world. It arises from the *Christian community*; theological education is a mutual process requiring participation in a community of students and teachers. It is *an ongoing process* which can never be completed; means must therefore be provided for continuing theological education.

In the next few chapters we shall be concerned chiefly with what goes on in theological schools, and so primarily with the training of professional ministers. But we must look at this training in the light of what has been said above, and we must also look at it in the context of the education of the whole people of God. Since the majority of theological students, at present, intend to seek full-time employment as professional ministers, we must ask (in Chapter 7) what professional education for ministers involves. There is every indication that the ministry of the future will be more diversified than the present, and this we must take into account. We must not forget, either, that there will be great changes in society and in the Church during the thirty or forty years of professional activity to which they now look forward. It may be that as a result of these changes some of them may find themselves doing quite different things from what they now expect.

We shall then look, in Chapter 8, at the structure of theological education, concentrating particularly on relations with universities and on ecumenical structures. We shall go on to look, in Chapter 9, at theological education outside the theological school through involvement in the structures of society. In Chapter 10, we shall discuss the curriculum of the theological school, asking how it is to be constructed, and what should be its integrating principle. Finally, in Chapter 11, we shall consider the theological school as a community, and ask whether it is the kind of community in which men and women can be trained for Christian living and for Christian ministry in the world today. A final chapter, as mentioned above, will look once more at the theological education of the whole people of God.

7 · Professional Education for Ministers

What is the difference between education and training? According to the dictionary, *education* aims at developing the moral and intellectual faculties of the individual, in order to broaden his knowledge of the world, and to make him able to deal with the situations he is likely to face. *Training*, on the other hand, aims at the development of skill in the performance of repetitive tasks, rather than reasoning ability. A lecturer in textile technology at Manchester University reminded a consultation of theological teachers in 1966 that 'many of the difficulties encountered in developing sound educational policies have arisen not from the mistaken view that general education is better than vocational training, but from the even more serious mistake of overlooking that there is such a thing as *vocational education*—education arranged with the prospective occupation of the student in mind'. Vocational education may include vocational training as an integral part of it, or the training may be given later during apprenticeship; but since education must be selective, there is a good deal to be said for making a selection of subjects with the future vocation in mind.

Such vocational education is not necessarily narrow. The vocational education of textile technologists at Manchester University includes subjects from every faculty except medicine and theology, and technological subjects form only about one third of the course. The basic principles on which such a course should be constructed are:

a that it must provide a complete education fitting the student to be a man in society, as a citizen and as a family man;

b that the subjects other than those forming the basic general education should be chosen with the future occupation of the student in mind;

c that it should include any training which is important for the prospective career of the student and which he will not otherwise receive.[1]

In the discussion which followed the members of the Consultation did not hesitate to apply these principles to theological education, understood as the 'training' of a professional ministry. Many of them were perhaps surprised at the extent to which the educational element preponderated over the element of training in the course which was being described. In an age when increasingly technologists are being *educated*, they asked themselves whether we can afford to speak any longer as if ministers only needed training. How far are we concerned that ministers should have a complete education, fitting them to be men in society, citizens and family men?

Before we consider further the lessons of vocational or professional education for the education of ministers, we must consider the implications of what we said in Part I about ministers as professionals. The use of the term 'vocational' as an alternative hardly helps. To say the ministry is a 'vocation' but not a 'profession', is to make a theological distinction which is irrelevant to the educational issue. In ordinary language, a 'vocation' is a 'career' and no theological implications remain. Professional and vocational education mean the same thing. From the point of view of the other professions, such as medicine, law or teaching, textile technology or business management, the ministry is a profession, and theological education is a professional education, even though it only partly understands itself in this way. We must remember, too, that in all the professions, research and scholarship in their particular field are fully as important as the education of future practitioners. Not all theologians become professional ministers—but then neither do all doctors or technologists practise their professions, although in most cases, and this is true of theologians too, they must be licensed to practise their profession before being admitted to teach it.

But our doubts in an earlier chapter did not just relate to the nature of theology as a study in its own right, but to the professional function of the ministry, and to the distinguishing mark, if any, separating the minister from the layman. We saw that professional ministers continue to be necessary in the churches, but that their professional tasks are likely to vary increasingly. This is true, too, of other professions in so far as increasing specialization seems to be a general law. But whereas in medicine, for instance, the tendency is towards a large number of distinct but related specialisms, this is only partly true of the ministry. Specialist ministers are needed with specialized training, but their specialisms are by no means so distinct: and besides there is another kind of variation described in our opening chapter, which is not functional at all. The tasks of ministers vary and will probably vary more in the future, but many of these tasks are hardly professional tasks. The professional character of the ministry, as we have seen, is not to be defined in terms of the particular tasks which ministers do but in terms of the way they perform certain general functions, in which all Christians have a share.

Certain tasks indeed fall frequently to the professional minister—preaching sermons, visiting the sick, conducting worship—in these a professional skill may be developed on the basis of certain knowledge and informed practice. Other tasks may increasingly be required—the leadership of small groups, the setting up of training programmes, the acting as chaplain or theological resource-person to a wide variety of social structures, not necessarily created by the churches. Here too professional skills can be developed and norms of professional conduct can be established. Perhaps, however, it is in the learning of professional attitudes, and in the learning, too, of how to work in a professional team, that the education of the minister should most closely resemble that of the other professions. Since, as a matter of fact, a somewhat similar change has been going on in many of them, and attention today is often directed to attitudes and team-work far more than to acquiring particular skills or performing precisely determined functions, the amount to be learnt from them is not negligible. There is a sense, indeed, in which the changes and development of theological education have not kept pace with the changes in other forms of professional education, simply because attention has been primarily fixed on developments in the field of theological scholarship. Other professions, and notably medicine, have possibly suffered in the same way, little thought, till recently, being devoted to the way practitioners may best learn the knowledge and skills required.

Lessons from Other Professions

The Episcopal Theological School in Cambridge, Massachusetts, held in January 1967, as part of its centennial celebrations, a Convocation on Graduate Professional Education, at which four leading educators in professional education in law, teaching, medicine and business respectively spoke not about theological education as it is or ought to be but about recent advances in the theory and practice of professional education in the USA in their own field. The papers were carefully prepared and annotated and contain material of the greatest interest. There are close parallels between some of the problems faced by education in these professions and those faced by theological education. A consideration of the trends and innovations in each case is therefore of value. The salient points are as follows.[2]

In *legal* education, according to Professor David P. Cavers of the Harvard Law School, there is a trend away from teaching legal doctrine towards the study of legal processes: judicial, legislative and administrative. This is facilitated by the case-method with its emphasis on the process of decision-making. This trend has made it easier to make curricular changes, and to avoid the pitfall of increasing the subject-matter by attempting to keep pace with the proliferation of laws and legal claims. Student discontent has led to providing more opportunities for research by individual students, and to the introduction of more diversity in the courses offered.

Another interesting development has been the involvement of students and of law schools in social responsibility, as for instance by the founding of a law office staffed by students in a poverty-stricken area of Cambridge. When this was started 250 students volunteered to take part in this programme.

Till recently the professional education of *teachers* concentrated on the teaching of 'professionalized subject-matter'. Courses on literature, psychology or the history of education, made a pre-selection of material directly relevant to the class-room and the school curriculum. This resulted in considerable distortion and in the alienation of professors of education from other members of the university community. Now, according to Professor Merle L. Borrowman of the University of Wisconsin School of Education, the trend has been reversed and there has been a mutual gain. On the other hand professors of education tend now to turn the practical side of teacher education over to the schools. A second problem relates to the professional expertise of the teacher which to some extent has consisted of skills and knowledge shared by a large number of parents. There has been a tendency to professionalize these skills, but this professionalization has inevitably reduced the possibilities of communication between the teacher and the public which he serves. A third area of tension, similar to that in other professions, is that of increased specialization, which may result in the abandonment of the one-teacher class-room.

In *medical* education, there have, in recent years, been a number of very significant curricular experiments. The most radical of these is that conducted in Western Reserve University, Cleveland, Ohio.[3] A new curriculum was planned and brought into operation on the basis of 'subject areas' instead of the usual departmental divisions. All departments co-operate in the teaching of a curriculum covering three phases: the study of normal structure and function, the study of disease, and the study of the patient. Medical students have been given blocks of free time and the basic concept, in the words of Dr. Peter V. Lee of the University of Southern California, has been 'that the faculty was concerned with the medical student as an individual person, maturing, well motivated, intelligent, who can take an increasing amount of responsibility for his own education—the student is the focal point of medical education'.

In *business* education the main feature has been the overwhelming success of the 'case-method' taken over and developed from legal education. 'The student is asked to put himself in the position of the responsible manager (retaining his own values, perception and judgement), to analyse the problem, and decide how he would try to deal with it. He is expected to seek out the information he needs, to apply the analytical methods he knows (and realize the need for others he will therefore learn later), apply his judgement to the alternatives he identifies, and make and defend his choice.'

'The outcome of two years of this exercise', according to Professor Kenneth W. Andrews of the Harvard Business School, 'is truly impressive. The student develops unmistakeable analytical power' and 'becomes accustomed to taking the initiative in his studies and his class discussion'. While for the faculty member, 'the teaching of complex cases to which there is no established answer appears to ward off faculty boredom, insularity, and obsolescence, and to foster intellectual growth'.

For the business school as for other professional schools, the 'information explosion' and the need to specialize creates a curricular problem which may be solved in several possible ways. The whole curriculum might consist of a succession of case-studies, but this is unsatisfactory. Harvard recently decided to 'give students environmental, mathematical and behavioural studies first, developing and illustrating concepts of analysis which will then be later applied to situations and decisions'. It may however be better in the end to reverse the order, or to develop theory and its application to particular cases side by side. Professor Andrews says: 'The motives and needs of professional students are so clear and the amount of relevant knowledge so vast, that we are well advised, I believe, to teach what we teach in the context of its use from the beginning.'

This brief summary of four important papers is sufficient to indicate the number of lessons relevant to the concerns of theological education which may be drawn from other professional fields. In an article on this theme, Owen C. Thomas, Professor of Theology at ETS and the organizer of the Convocation, notes certain points with obvious relevance to theological education,[4] which may be listed as follows:

1 Most of the professions regard the university as the necessary place for professional education; theological education is normally carried on in seminaries.
2 Most professional schools recognize the need for practical training and take some responsibility for it; theological education is undecided whether this should be the job of the schools or of the churches, and does not distinguish clearly between the theory of practice and training in practice.
3 There is a general tendency in professional education towards an inductive methodology with much use of the case and problem method; theological education is far behind in teaching methodology.
4 The question of specialization is a problem for all professions in a day when the typical professional is a specialist member of a team or group practice; there is some experience in other professions of relating a basic professional education to later specialization which might be copied by theological education.

As a final point, Thomas notes that 'a continuing problem in the professions is their mutual relations', a problem which is evidently of importance for the ministry. 'This raises', he says, 'the intriguing possibility of a measure of joint education in the professions. This might be of two types: in areas of mutual concern or of occasional cooperation, and in areas where professional persons perform similar but independent functions. As examples of the former, theological students might join medical students in classes in ethics and specific moral problems. Examples of the latter derive from the fact

83

that the minister occasionally has to perform the functions of a teacher or a manager. Thus a theological student might spend a certain amount of time in a school of education or a business school.'

A Functional Approach

The approach taken by vocational or professional education as described in the first part of the chapter, can be termed a *functional* approach. It is geared to the function for which the student is being prepared. Practical training, however, forms only a small part of professional education. More important than the learning of practical skills, or even than the assimilation of detailed knowledge in the field of study, is the learning of an appropriate methodology, the approach to an integrated understanding of what is being done and why, and the acquiring of professional attitudes of thoroughness, systematic analysis and responsibility. From this point of view, a technological education which only taught a man how to run machines, a medical education which was only concerned with the treating of particular diseases, or an education for teachers imparting nothing but 'professionalized subject-matter' would not be functional at all. Functionalism implies an integrated educational approach; it is increasingly seen to imply an inductive methodology which starts from where the student is; it does not imply a concentration on practical training.

This point is made strongly with regard to theological education, by Keith Bridston in his paper prepared for the WCC Study and entitled 'Form and Function in the Education of Ministers'.[5] He sees the introduction of 'practical' or 'functional' courses in theological education (a process which has gone further in the USA than anywhere else) as an attempt to introduce the wrong kind of functional relevance, an attempt which has inevitably resulted in dividing the curriculum into 'academic' and 'practical' courses. A course in pastoral counselling or Christian education is no more functional than one in Church history or dogmatics. Rather, 'the criterion for judging whether a particular educational programme is functional or not is not the explicit how-to-do-it character which it exhibits but whether the education is *organically* related to the actual demands of the professional practice and is thus, in this *integrated* way, functional'.

In the above quotation I have italicized the two key words which describe the kind of functionalism that Bridston wants. To quote the Report of the American study group for which Bridston's paper was written: 'If all educational disciplines become oriented towards giving today's ministers what they will need and in the way which they need it, the results would be an *organically* articulated unity. . . . Such a demand for *organic* unification will involve internal changes in objective and method in many a classroom. . . . A third clue for a new concept of organically integrated unity in theological education' is 'the role played in the educational process by the student himself as *person*.'[6] Keith Bridston illustrates his argument by quoting the writings of the American architect, Frank Lloyd Wright, many of whose works adorn the city of Berkeley, California, where Bridston teaches. Wright's famous dictum, 'Form follows function', was quickly misunderstood by his followers who interpreted his functionalism too narrowly. 'When we say "form and function are one", ' wrote the architect, 'only then do we take mere fact into the realm of creative thought. I should say that in that difference of statement lies the real difference between organic work, and that of professed functionalism.'[7]

On what basis is an 'organically functional' theological education to be constructed? What, we must ask once more, is the function of the minister? To this question, as we have seen, there is no clear answer. We cannot define a minister's function in the precise way we should like to. In an earlier chapter we have shown that a minister may have to perform many functions; that there are different kinds of ministry requiring different specialist knowledge; that the essential function of the minister can only be described in the most general terms, which do not clearly differentiate him from the layman. Does this mean, then, that a functional education of any kind is excluded?

To arrive at this conclusion is in fact to commit the error identified above. It is a narrow functionalism which would concentrate on teaching preachers homiletics, priests liturgics, and pastoral directors parish organization. An organic functionalism in medical education (as at Western Reserve Medical School) will strive to form doctors who understand the nature of health and disease and their own role in society as medical men. An organic functionalism in business education (as at Harvard Business School) will aim at educating students to the point where they can solve new problems by bringing to bear their powers of analysis and by knowing where to look for such information as may be relevant. And so in theological education the curriculum should not be geared to the particular tasks a minister may be called upon to do, but to the general and more basic functions of the ministry. A minister's education must help him achieve a maximum degree of *theological awareness* together with the ability to communicate it to others; an understanding of what *Christian presence* means, and the will and courage to seek to be present in this way; the desire to *serve men* according to the best of his ability, and the catholic vision and love which will show him where and how they need to be served.

How is this to be done? Bridston, in this essay and elsewhere, takes as an analogy the training of the psychiatrist, who must himself undergo psychological analysis before he is fit to analyse others. 'In theological education', he says, 'the abstract, scientific theological truths must become existentially immediate to the candidate. There must be a break-through into the unconscious of the various theological and dogmatic insights and precepts. Formal theology must become interiorized'.[8] This process, to which he gives the colourful title of 'theoanalysis', is the basic element in theological education. It is this which give the student a theology he can use, making available for his future ministry both the information he has learnt and skills he has acquired, and at the same time helping him through the professional identity crisis, which is so acute for the theological student—and particularly acute today. It helps him to come to terms with himself and to come to terms with the world, and so to reach that 'professional piety' which will enable him to serve others and bear witness to them of the presence of Christ in the world.

According to Bridston, Roman Catholic seminaries with their insistence on 'spiritual formation' have been relatively successful in this task. Pope Pius X compared the seminary to a workshop where weapons for battle are forged. The Roman Catholic Church has taken care that its professional leaders should be ideologically informed. Protestants have not understood this need so clearly, and yet the traditional Protestant concentration on content courses has perhaps achieved more in the direction of ideological crystallization, than in its avowed aim of imparting information. What is certain is that, in a new situation, new methods are required. The patterns of fifty years ago will serve no longer. No longer do students come to the theological schools versed in the content of the Christian faith and fully committed to practising it. Theological teachers complain about the first deficiency, but the second is even more important; nor is it surprising in an age when theological questioning is going on more widely than ever before. The Northwood Consultation pointed to this fact and affirmed, as Bridston does, that theological education must start with the student as he is.[9]

The term 'theoanalysis' does not imply the use of group or individual psychotherapy. The psychoanalytic method is 'a parallel or model, not a substitute for theological training'. There are various ways in which theological education can be made to fit the model. Bridston himself uses the case-study method, teaching Christian doctrine by discussing with his students the theological implications of typical pastoral problems as encountered by parish ministers in their work. In this discussion the students discover how the theology they have learnt ties up with real life. At the same time, by exposing their own judgements and attitudes to the criticism of their fellow students, they discover, too, that beneath their formal theological positions they have theological preconceptions and inhibitions which may be inconsistent with them. In this way they reach a mature

87

theological awareness not only of the world but of themselves and resolve the crisis of their professional identity.

A method such as this can take advantage of social and cultural differences in different areas and can be developed at different educational levels. Bridston himself first used it in Indonesia in the attempt to bridge the cultural and ideological gaps separating him from his students. In later chapters we shall have occasion to refer to experiments and methods of teaching designed for the same purpose. Without accepting Bridston's thesis in all particulars, we can agree that it is in some such way as this that theological education must be structured if it is to prepare students for the kind of ministry described in the first part of the book.

8 · The Structure of Theological Education

Current discussion on theological education tends to focus on two points: (1) the value of study in a university setting, and (2) the need for theological teaching to be put on an ecumenical basis. Both points, if taken seriously, imply considerable changes from the present situation; since, though much theological education is conducted in a university, much is not, and most theological education takes place on a confessional rather than on an ecumenical basis.

Both of these points appear among the recommendations of the Northwood Consultation,[1] and they figure repeatedly in the many recent studies on theological education conducted by different churches. The trend of the discussion, in fact, seems to point this way, but counter-arguments also carry weight, and there is a certain reluctance to translate theory into practice. It is much easier for a particular school to introduce changes in its curriculum or teaching methods, than for a church to change the whole structure of theological education. It is not always easy, indeed, to see how such changes can be introduced, since theological education is frequently the responsibility of a number of different bodies. Neither the churches, nor the theological schools themselves, may be in a position to initiate change without the agreement of other parties such as the universities, private foundations, or the State. Many of the schemes described in this chapter and in the next, excellent as they may seem on paper, have yet to be put into effect, and may have to be modified before this happens because of the difficulty of reaching the necessary agreement. Although at times there may seem to be a certain inertia in the whole system of theological education, this is by no means always the fault of the churches, or of theological educators themselves (though sometimes, of course, it may be). In many cases, and especially in Europe, the system has slowly developed over the years, without any very marked control on the part of the churches, and now that change is desired, vested interests may make change extremely difficult.

Change is certainly desired. It is desired by many ministers, and by many theological educators. It is desired by the students. It is desired also by many churches, as is evident from the number of studies on theological education referred to in the previous paragraph. Most of these antedate the study by the World Council of Churches, and have contributed not a little to it. That study was initiated in 1964, at the request of the New Delhi Assembly, which met three years previously. Already for ten years the World Council had been under some pressure to set up such a study, and had indeed taken some steps in that direction, which could not, however, be followed up for lack of funds and personnel. The discussion in Germany, in India, in the United States, in Great Britain and in Africa got under way in the fifties and by 1964 had gathered momentum. When a survey of current discussion was published in the first issue of *Ministry*,[2] early in 1965, it was possible to refer to studies then in progress in many churches in over twenty countries. Since then the number has increased considerably, and some of the earlier studies have been published.[3]

None of these studies have concluded that all is well with theological education and that no major changes need to be made. On the contrary, in a very large number of them, the two points listed above have been central. Where theological education has been conducted in denominational schools, close co-operation is urged with similar schools of other churches, and, even more frequently, it is recommended that links should be forged with adjacent universities. Even where theological education is already conducted in a university setting, and on an ecumenical basis, it is stressed that such relationships need strengthening and, perhaps, reformulation, in the light of recent thinking on the ministry and of the changed ecumenical climate. Even in those cases where a university link might seem, to the outside observer, to be more of a disadvantage than an advantage, it is never, to my knowledge, maintained that such a link should be broken. Similarly, although certain structures of ecumenical co-operation in theological education have proved unsound and transitory, I know of no church which has given up the attempt to bring workable ecumenical structures into being.

Theological education is at the point of change. The general directions of the changes are beginning to be clear. What is unclear is how the change is to be made. For this reason, we must consider in some detail the reasons for the changes which are recommended, together with some of the proposals for carrying them out. Questions of curricula and teaching method will be considered later.

Theological Education in the University

Starting with the university link, where this is possible, the advantages are considerable. There is, *firstly*, the fact that a university, by reason of its size, standing and public character (including its access to public funds), is able to provide more adequate educational resources than any other institution. As compared with most independent or church-related schools, universities have better libraries, more opportunities for research and post-graduate study, larger teaching staffs with a wider variety of special interests and with different points of view. Further they are able to apply to the theological field educational experience and teaching methods developed elsewhere; and they may be able to offer courses in other faculties which are of importance for theological students. Only the exceptional 'theological university' with ample endowments can match these provisions, and even there a link with other university institutions will be of advantage.[4]

There is, *secondly*, the question of standards. The other professions look to the universities for professional education, not just because of the educational resources mentioned above, but because, as things are, a university education is the best guarantee of demanding, objective and consistent standards, both as regards the qualifications of teaching staff, and as regards the admission and graduation of students. A profession can of course set up its own standards—many have done so—but the university link is a public guarantee that the standards of one profession are in line with those of others. In the case of the ministry there is a peculiar difficulty since denominational divisions prevent the development of standards of professional education nationally recognized. There is also the problem that in many churches the scarcity of university-trained ministers or ministerial candidates tends to pull down the standards of entry demanded by the denomination, and only the university link can put pressure on the denomination to maintain its standards or even to raise them.

The formation of associations of theological schools in different parts of the world, especially where theological education is not carried on in universities, helps provide a pressure on churches and theological schools to keep on raising their standards until they are on a par with other institutions of higher education. Much has been achieved in this way both in the USA and in South-East Asia. Such associations can also to some extent lessen the disadvantages of the smaller school, for example, by running regular institutes for teachers in particular fields, or by developing graduate schools jointly between a number of institutions which may be at some distance from each other and may belong to different churches.[5]

A *third* advantage of the university link (which these associations can also, in part, provide) is that theological education can then achieve a certain independence of church control. Theology in the past has often been taught dogmatically, in seminaries and faculties related to particular confessions. Open enquiry has been frowned upon; the doubts and questions of students have been put aside, and a certain pressure to conform has been brought on them, no less effective because it is indirect and usually unintentional. Most theological schools today are aware of this risk, and do their best to avoid it. While some are successful in this, in others, often the smaller ones with least academic pretensions, an uneasy balance is struck between the spirit of free enquiry and the claims of revealed religion. The churches are naturally anxious that their ministers should have a thorough grasp of Christian truth, and that they should personally appropriate it on the basis of faith and deep conviction. They have sometimes, however, gone about the task in the wrong way, and have not recognized the integrity and openness proper to an educational institution.

Here an analogy may be helpful. It is generally recognized that the State has a duty to develop and maintain the university system. Clearly a university education is of great benefit to its citizens, and indirectly to the State itself. But the universities, in spite of state support, claim an autonomy in what they teach and the way they teach it. Where pressure is applied to conform, either through the dissemination of an official ideology, or through the appointment or dismissal of certain professors, the universities will consider this an infringement of their rights, and, with more or less success, oppose it. The theological school should have a similar autonomy with respect to the churches (also of course with respect to the universities and to the State!); it should encourage students to ask questions, to express their doubts, and to discover their own personal conviction. It should encourage its teachers to be open to the truth, wherever it may lead, and to be critical if need be of the teaching and practice of the churches.

In recent discussion, this necessary characteristic of theological education—its integrity and openness to the truth—has figured largely. In one place it is described as 'rigour'.[6] This should be seen 'as equivalent to the scholar's intellectual integrity: the truth must be pursued with all the resources at the student's command, even though he is personally committed to belief in God who is ultimately the subject of the document he is studying'. Such an attitude must be applied not only to the traditional subject-matter of theology but to the pressures and questionings of secular life. It involves both 'a rigorous refusal to allow any part of theology to become merely academic', and 'a rigorous openness' to the world.

Rigour requires a degree of autonomy, an autonomy most easily guaranteed by a university link, even when this is an external one. A church may retain primary responsibility for running its own institutions but where a university curriculum and university examinations are adopted, where teaching appointments may be shared and students are free to attend university classes, the university's own standards of free enquiry are imposed on the theological school, and limit to some extent the control of the church on the content and method of teaching. The voluntary acceptance of membership in an association of theological schools will have the same effect, and may be preferable in situations where the university is itself subject to pressure from outside. After all, the autonomy of the university is not complete, as is shown by recent European history. It is interesting, in view of this, that theological educators on the continent of Europe are almost unanimous in holding that, wherever possible, theological education should continue to be carried on largely in the open forum of the secular university.[7]

In part, this is true because of the *fourth* advantage of the university link, the one least easily supplied by any other arrangement, and possibly, the most convincing. A university is still, by definition, a place where different disciplines are studied. It consists of several faculties, of which theology is only one. Or it may be that theology is taught within the Faculty of Arts or of Social Science. In any case it forms only a part of the spectrum of knowledge covered by the university. By this fact, it is brought into close contact with study and research in other fields of human endeavour. Unless, as sometimes happens, the theological professor and the theological student withdraw into their own particular ivory tower, dialogue and debate can take place between theology and other subjects. Students are exposed to teaching on different presuppositions from their own; they are obliged to defend their views to their fellow-students and may learn something of what they believe and what they study.

All this of course does not take place in every instance, but it can take place better in the university than anywhere else. Theological schools and theological teachers can take more opportunities than perhaps they have done in the past to stimulate this encounter, to initiate dialogue to show their students the relevance to theological studies of historical, linguistic and sociological enquiry, and to point out to their colleagues in other fields the implications of theology for the study of philosophy, politics and literature. A particular opportunity is present—and it may be thought also a particular danger—when Christian theology or some aspects of it is taught alongside the theology or phenomenology of another religion. Here may take place an inter-religious dialogue, as in some universities in North America, in Africa or in Japan. Or again there may be the opportunity for dialogue with a secular ideology like Marxism or scientific humanism. In such a situation there may indeed be a considerable limitation on what may or may not legitimately be taught in a university class-room. It is unlikely that a complete theological education for professional ministry can be carried on there, but the advantages of such an encounter are so great, that every effort should be made to encourage it.

It cannot of course be said that the advantages of a university link will always outweigh the disadvantages. Too great a limitation on freedom may be imposed. Again, there are some cases where universities are excluded from teaching Christian theology, or where a confessional theology of only one kind may be allowed. In such situations churches of other confessions will have no alternative but to establish their own theological schools. Again there may be other cases where the standards of university education are lower than those which the churches demand.

Again, not all ministerial candidates are capable of study at university level, though they may have other gifts which would make them excellent ministers. It is therefore unrealistic to plead for the education of *all* ministers to take place in universities, or in university-linked institutions. It is possible, however, to demand that the structure of theological education as a whole, in any particular church, should be in 'critical relationship with the surrounding educational system'.[8] Normally the relationship will be with a university or universities. Some examples are given below.

A link already exists between University Departments of Religious Studies in Ghana, Nigeria and Uganda and adjacent theological colleges of several denominations, permitting students who are candidates for the Bachelor of Arts degree to prepare for ordination in these colleges. For these students their university courses are considered to form a major part of their theological education; other students in the same colleges will follow a different course unrelated to university requirements. A similar arrangement is proposed for University College, Nairobi, where a Department of Religious Studies is to be established. In all these cases Christianity is only one of the religions studied at the University and the course for ordinands also includes a study of Islam and African religion as well as courses in the Departments of African Studies. A similar relationship exists between the United Theological College of the West Indies and the University of the West Indies, in Kingston, Jamaica, and one is proposed between the Pacific Theological College, Suva, Fiji, and the new University of the South Pacific. In each case the theological colleges concerned are on adjacent sites to the universities or have moved to such sites to permit easy association. The colleges retain their autonomy and are not committed to a permanent relationship, if the current mood of the university should change; nor are they bound in any way only to admit graduating students.

In Germany, Scandinavia, Switzerland and the Netherlands, the faculties of theology in the state universities have till fairly recently provided the whole theological education for ministers of the majority Lutheran and Reformed churches, though, in most cases the examinations have been conducted by joint commissions on which the churches have had representatives. In Germany, since the end of the last century, most theological graduates have been required to work for a period in a local parish and to attend a supplementary course at a church seminary (*Predigerseminar*) before sitting their second and final examination. Similar provisions have been introduced in Holland and Denmark since the Second World War, and are being considered in Sweden and Switzerland. The churches have had some say in the appointment of professors but almost none in what was taught or the way it was taught, and the supplementary courses at the seminaries have, in consequence, been less efficient than they might have been. Now, in all these countries, the course of theological education, on the whole, is being jointly studied by representatives of the faculties and of the churches, and there are signs that a new and more intimate relationship will, in certain cases, be proposed so that the educational resources of church and university may be more efficiently related.[9] For most ministers, theological education will certainly continue to be conducted in a university. It is likely, however, that the churches will be constrained to take further such experiments as have already been made in courses for students unable to enter a theological faculty,[10] because they have not been able to complete their secondary education or have studied the wrong subjects.

In the Church of England there has been considerable discussion in recent years on the best relationship between the theological colleges and the university faculties or departments of theology. It has now been accepted by the English Bishops, on the advice of ACCM (The Advisory Council for the Church's Ministry) that all ordinands who are not graduates in theology should spend some part of their theological training at a university, reading for a degree or diploma in theology, and that the whole period of theological education for these men should normally take three years. At least two years of this period should be spent in residence at a theological college, which would no longer need to give them instruction in all branches of theology (since some of this would be covered in a university course).

Each of these patterns assumes a continued willingness on the part of society to allow Christian theology or some aspects of it to be taught in the universities. As we have seen, this situation does not obtain in every country, and the mood of society or of the universities may change. Where it does obtain, however, there is often more goodwill now to the academic study of theology than there was fifty or a hundred years ago, and there is a greater readiness, than sometimes the churches are aware of, to go beyond the historical and linguistic approach to theological studies characteristic for long of the European universities. Joint honours courses of theology and sociology, as at the University of Bristol; institutes of liturgy and architecture, as at Birmingham; post-graduate diplomas in pastoral studies, as at Birmingham and Edinburgh—these are indications in one country of a readiness to adapt to the needs of the contemporary Church. They are also indications that the university can, in some instances, provide the kind of professional training which ministers require as part of their professional education. It is interesting, too, that in Germany, where practical theology has been very much the step-sister of the other disciplines, the suggestion has now been made by a student group, and welcomed by many professors, that practical theology should be seen as the central discipline relating historical and systematical theology to each other and to the empirical reality of Church and society as seen by the social sciences. In place of the *Predigerseminar*, the church-related institution which attempted at a later stage to perform this integrating task, the authors of this memorandum propose a university institute of practical theology which would include in the early years of the course, periods of social work and vocational training which would then be the subject of theological reflection.[11]

Ecumenical Structure

University theological education is already to some extent ecumenical, in the sense that what is taught cannot just be the theology of one particular denomination. Already for many decades the academic study of theology has ignored denominational boundaries. Biblical, historical and systematic theology alike have been pursued, like other university studies, in a world community. Till recently, perhaps, the line between Protestant and Catholic theology has remained relatively firm. Today this is no longer true. No course of reading for any theological subject is limited to authors from one confession.

In another sense too, universities are ecumenical, since, though one tradition may be dominant in a given university, there will be students and increasingly teachers from other traditions too; this may indeed be a legal requirement. And yet, for that very reason, students may not be aware of the true nature of the ecumenical dialogue, since everything that has to do with the particular beliefs of the different churches is soft-pedalled, and there is no frank discussion of what unites the churches and what divides them. In the present ecumenical situation, this effortless ecumenism is hardly sufficient. Something more positive is required; something which the universities very often are not able to provide. If it is to be provided, if that solid and demanding ecumenical education is to take place which is the only hope for the continued life and growth of the Ecumenical Movement, then it is the churches that must provide it.

How is this to be done? What ecumenical structures are required in the field of theological education? What place in these structures should be given to the existing denominational theological colleges? For in the present situation it is the separate denominational schools that must justify their continued existence, and not the new ecumenical structures that are beginning to emerge. It no longer makes any sense for a school to attempt to teach theology 'ecumenically', if only one denomination is represented among its students. If the churches are committed to an ecumenical approach, to do together what does not need to be done separately, then theological education is clearly one of the most important things which must be done together. Today's theological students may find themselves working at some future date in a united church.

Should they not then as students learn to understand the theology and practice of those churches with which their own church is currently in conversation? And even where union seems more distant, there is surely much to gain if the whole or part of the theological course is done in common by future ministers of churches which are ecumenically involved in study and action together.

And yet although the churches may be committed to this it is not easy to move from their present separate theological establishments to the kind of ecumenical theological education they desire. Several patterns, indeed, are possible. One of these is the *union* college, and there are many of these, in Asia and Africa, but also in North America. It is interesting that in recent unions more care has been taken than previously to ensure the continued presence of elements in the separate institutional life of the uniting colleges. Whereas earlier union colleges tended to become 'interdenominational', and to turn out ministers of undifferentiated churchmanship who were most at home in union congregations; some of the newer unions emphasize to a far greater extent the specific contributions of the various participating denominations, in terms of confessional theology, worship and spirituality.

An alternative pattern is the *federal* one where the separate schools come together to share their educational resources but do not merge their separate identities. This pattern which has developed in the States, especially at the graduate level, for example in Berkeley, California, is being widely hailed as the pattern of the future, especially where it is combined with the university link.[12] In the last year or two several American seminaries have announced the establishment of such relationships, or a projected move to a new site which would make such a relationship possible. It is now indeed the avowed policy of the American Association of Theological Schools to encourage the formation of seminary 'clusters'. The Resources Planning Commission of the Association has recently made public[13] a proposal to redevelop American theological education entirely on this basis. In each cluster the seminaries would retain their separate institutional identity but would function together for all educational purposes, and would be jointly linked to a nearby university.

These are not necessarily the only possible patterns. An open university with a theological faculty not related to any particular confession provides, as we have seen, a minimum ecumenical setting for theological education but one that needs to be supplemented. The usual way of doing this has been for the churches to expect students subsequently to attend a denominational seminary, but this has its disadvantages. One proposal, made in the States, suggests that instead students should receive supplementary confessional instruction at non-residential houses of study during their university education.[14] This might be more effective.

Again, if separate churches were prepared to recognize the standards and teaching of theological colleges in other denominations, it would be possible for more frequent and regular exchange of students and staff to take place between theological schools. Some churches already value the possibility of such exchanges through the Ecumenical Scholarships Programme of the World Council of Churches, which in the past has tended to take candidates to another country as well as to another church. But there is no reason why the churches in Britain, for example, might not arrange their own internal exchange scheme so that it became normal for a minister of the Church of Scotland to have spent a term or even a year in an Anglican college, or for an Anglican priest to have studied for some time in a Baptist or Methodist one. Possibilities exist of similar exchanges with Roman Catholic and Orthodox institutions, and should certainly be developed. Again the practice should be commended of theological schools of one denomination appointing members of other churches to teach theology from their own confessional point of view, and so to provide an ecumenical stimulus to both staff and students. In the last year or two several Roman Catholic and Protestant seminaries in the USA have exchanged staff members in this way to their mutual profit.

Finally, we may ask if there is not a case for the foundation of one or two theological schools which are ecumenical from the start, so to speak, and are not mergers of schools previously existing. An example of such a school would be the Theological College of Lanka in Ceylon or the Pacific Theological School, mentioned above. The Nottingham Faith and Order Conference in 1964 specifically called for the formation of such an ecumenical college in Great Britain. The recent approval by the churches concerned of the plan whereby Queen's College, Birmingham, will in due course admit students from the Methodist Church (and eventually from other churches) as well as Anglican ordinands, is most encouraging.

9 · Theological Education outside the Theological School

Theological education does not only take place in institutions. Most candidates for the Christian ministry spend some time in practical training, usually in a local church. In some cases, the arrangement and supervision of this training is undertaken by the theological school. More generally, perhaps, it is the responsibility of the church. Often there is inadequate provision for its integration into the whole educational programme. Yet this integration is of paramount importance. As we have seen, a professional education which is truly functional must be an integrated education and this integration must include whatever elements of vocational training may be required. Clearly, it is the responsibility of the church, and not just of the theological school, to see that this is so.

In fact several different kinds of vocational training are required. In 'Education for Ministry',[1] the report of a North American study on Education for the Practice of the Parish Ministry, Professor Charles Feilding of Toronto distinguishes four stages of practical training which would successively help the student to test (1) his vocation as a Christian, (2) his vocation to the (ordained) ministry, (3) his capacity to minister, and (4) his aptitude for specialization. To some extent these stages merge into each other, and we shall not separate them completely in our discussion. Stage 1 is the most important. It is equally appropriate for students not intending to enter the professional ministry. It will normally not take place in a church structure or institution, and—for that reason—it is not often provided for, either by the churches or by theological schools. We shall discuss it under the heading: Secular Involvement. Stages 2 and 3 are forms of field education; we shall discuss them with particular reference to the concept of Supervision as developed in Clinical Pastoral Education; Stage 4 concerns Continuing Education and we shall discuss this last.

Secular Involvement

On Bridston's view, the major aim of theological education is to help the student relate his theology to his existential situation, as an individual and as a citizen of the contemporary world. This requires both some knowledge and some experience of that world, which in the cloistered community of a theological school he may easily avoid. This is particularly so where, as so often, the typical ministerial candidate comes from a devout Christian home and proceeds to theological study immediately on completing his secondary (or college) education. Practical field work in a local parish will not provide the experience which he needs. What is required is rather a period of involvement in a secular structure which is not primarily an institution of formal education. This 'secular confrontation' with the contemporary world should take place at an early stage in theological education. It is quite distinct from whatever in-service training may be required after formal education ends. Nor is it adequately achieved by the theoretical consideration of contemporary problems in the class-room or even by academic debate with humanists and men of other faiths in a university setting.[2]

For examples of such involvement as part of theological education we must turn in the first place to North America. In several schools 'exposure units' have been developed, whereby first-year Bachelor of Divinity degree students find themselves one day a week in a mental hospital, in the front seat of a police car or in a doss-house in a city slum. A longer period of involvement is provided in the courses for theological students arranged by the Urban Training Centre in Chicago and the Metropolitan Urban Service Training Facility (MUST) in New York.[3] The latter is really a form of the intern year which many American seminaries require. In this case, however, the student is not an intern in a local congregation, but is required to seek secular employment in New York City, to live with another student in a tenement apartment, and to join at least one community organization working for brotherhood or justice. His only ecclesiastical and educational commitments during the year are to attend regularly a city congregation and to give ten hours a week to corporate study and reflection with other interns on the experience they are undergoing.

Similar though shorter projects are operative in other parts of the world: in Asia—in Manila, Bangkok, Tainan and Osaka, Japan; in Africa—at Dar es Salaam; and in Latin America—in the River Plate region. In Europe, a year in a factory is increasingly required by German churches as a prerequisite for theological study. The field 'vacations' which form part of the training for priests in the *Mission de France* are somewhat similar, and frequently include the stipulation that the future priest should learn a secular trade. Other churches too are considering introducing this latter provision.

A comprehensive scheme for a co-ordinated structure of theological education has been suggested by the Curriculum Task Force of the American Association of Theological Schools. Following the recommendations of the earlier Bridston-Culver report on Pre-Seminary Education,[4] they postulate a tripartite division of the student's career. Level I (pre-seminary education) will take place at a university or undergraduate college; level II at the theological 'nucleus' formed by a cluster of denominational seminaries (an optimum size of 540 students and 53 faculties is recommended for the nucleus). This will have no specific professional orientation, but will be preceded by a summer vacation of 'direct involvement in one of the many arenas of crisis such as the urban scene or migratory workers, civil rights, farmer cooperatives, or labor unions'. This may well include secular employment; its aims would be: 'social understanding, personal involvement, with reflection on its meaning, and experience of group life'. Level III will consist of two alternative programmes, one of which (III B) is a doctoral programme aimed at theological teaching and research. Most candidates however will proceed to III A which will be conducted in one of a number of 'centres' linked to the 'nucleus', and together with it forming an educational 'cluster'.

The centres will not be formal educational institutions but will be structures similar to the MUST programme described above, but scattered throughout different social and geographical contexts. Each centre will have 25-35 students and 5-7 professional teachers (though part-time teachers will also be employed). Students will take secular employment and will 'live out' but will gather regularly for instruction and corporate reflection in quarters rented for the purpose. Such instruction will include lectures and discussions with professional and community leaders in the particular sector to which the centre is directed. A suggested list of such centres covers suburban, inner city and rural areas, the world of business, and of politics, 'crisis areas' (for example civil rights, poverty or war), and the world of the arts. Not every cluster will contain centres of all these kinds and more students will clearly opt for involvement in the inner city or in suburban problems than in the areas of business or the arts. The period of involvement (eleven months following on two years at Level II) would be carefully supervised and co-ordinated with Level II study, and methods would be developed for assessing progress and awarding credits.

It should be said that some American theological educators differ in seeing this essential period of secular involvement not as part of theological education but as a pre-condition for it. In a recent lecture the former dean of a major theological school asserted that the seminaries should no longer seek to provide that training for mature manhood which must precede the training for Christian ministry. Those who have not participated personally in the struggles of society ought not to be given leadership in the Church. At the present moment in American history the would-be seminarian must refuse to opt out from the moral burden which weighed on his contemporaries by accepting automatic exemption from military service.

Seminaries should require two years involvement in the social crises of mankind before admission to a theological course. This period might be spent in the Peace Corps or in equivalent social service; it might also be spent in jail, if the candidate renounces his exemption and refuses to serve in any form.[5]

Field Education

Under this heading we must look first of all at the growth of Clinical Pastoral Education, essentially an application to the theological field of a learning method used in the training of doctors. It is perhaps one of the most significant developments in theological education in recent years and has attracted a great deal of attention outside North America where it was first developed. Courses are now being held in Great Britain, Australia and the Netherlands, but only small numbers of students are so far involved. Many European students applying for ecumenical scholarships to the USA ask specifically to participate in such a course. The European student, and perhaps the theological educator as well, may be unaware of the controversy about CPE (as it is called) which exists in the States, due to the fact that it first developed outside the normal structure of theological education, and that this has intensified the gulf which already existed between the 'classical disciplines' and 'practical training'. For the European student, as for the American seminarian before him, the appeal of CPE is partly a result of his impatience with the theological education he has received, and the desire to do something which will be of 'real use to him later on'. It is also, no doubt, partly due to the secret attraction, mingled with dread, of a learning-situation which will challenge his faith and make him or break him as a Christian.

The history of CPE can be traced in Professor Feilding's report, and also in the paper by Theodore Bachmann prepared for the Washington Consultation entitled 'A New Approach to Field Education'. Both these documents make the important point that, quite apart from the merits of CPE as such, the concept and experience of *supervision* which has there emerged is a major methodological advance in theological education. This method can be applied far beyond the 'clinical' setting in which it has been developed (usually a mental hospital, a general hospital, or, in some cases, a prison). In 'Education for Ministry' there is a chapter on 'Supervision' written by Thomas W. Klink of the Menninger Foundation, Topeka, Kansas, a foremost practitioner of CPE.[6] His definition is as follows:

1 Supervision is a unique and identifiable educational procedure;
2 it requires as supervisor one who is both engaged in the practice of his profession and duly qualified to supervise;
3 it assumes as student a candidate seeking fuller qualification in the practice of his (intended) profession;
4 it requires for its setting an institution within whose activities there are functional roles in which student and supervisor can negotiate a 'contract of learning';
5 the roles of both supervisor and student must be appropriate to their particular professional identity (in this case the Christian ministry);
6 lastly, supervision requires for its environment a wider community of professional peers associated in a common task.

It is noteworthy that this definition does not specifically refer to the clinical setting. At a later point, Klink indicates further conditions for successful supervision which clearly obtain in such institutions but are not limited to them either. He describes supervision as 'a dynamic process' taking place in 'a period of anxiety' which arises from professional training; it implies 'a structure of activities and duties' appropriate to the objectives of the student's needs of the training institution; and it helps the student 'inform practice with knowledge' in a situation where both are available.

The concept of supervision has developed in clinical institutions for historical reasons, but also because chaplain-supervisors were already there to hand and functioned as members of therapeutic teams. Further, in such institutions, there was minimum interference from existing structures of church or seminary. Today, however, CPE no longer needs to justify itself in the eyes of these structures and closer links are being sought from both sides. The American Association of Theological Schools has been able to play a mediating role in this discussion, and has suggested criteria for administrative relationships between seminaries and the recognized centres of clinical training, as also for the awarding of academic credit, and for the selection of chaplain-supervisors.

According to Dr. Bachmann the methodology of CPE could transform the whole concept of field education—a form of professional education to be distinguished alike from 'field employment' (as a form of student support) and 'field service' (as a way of involving theological students in the Church's diaconia). For this to happen, professional standards must be introduced, careful supervision must take place, and the supervisors (be they pastors of local congregations, or specialist ministers) must be carefully trained. Some of the larger seminaries in the USA have developed such programmes which also serve to strengthen the bonds between seminary and local churches.[7] Such programmes are not easy to finance, since they require much time from the supervisors as well as from seminary staff, and since the students must, as a rule, be compensated for the field employment they would otherwise have taken. It is therefore highly desirable that the congregation should see this as an educational service which they and their pastors can perform, and not as a way in which they can get the part-time services of a student-assistant. The valuable part which can be played in supervision by lay members of the church should also be stressed. In every case the assignment of students to a particular congregation or pastor should depend on the possibility of adequate supervision and not on the need for an extra pair of hands, or alternatively on its organizational success.

Field education of this kind may belong to Feilding's Stage 2 or to Stage 3. If both are possible, the former should take place during the theological course and should involve a 'limited identification with ministerial roles'. A more prolonged period of in-service training after leaving the theological school is probably more essential and involves 'the progressive assumption of ministerial responsibility'. In practice this is normally arranged by the church rather than by the theological school. The important thing is that there should be some relation between what has been learnt at theological school and what happens afterwards; and equally that the in-service training should be regarded as part of the educational experience and should therefore be supervised. Some churches delay ordination till after this period is completed, and this is a good thing. It is also good if, as is sometimes done, such 'probationer ministers' are gathered together for brief periods at the beginning and end of their period of service for corporate reflection and for more formal instruction. In some German churches, where residence in a *Predigerseminar* has followed the *Vikarzeit*, this opportunity is already assured. Other churches, for example the Church of Scotland and the Reformed Church of France, have only recently introduced such a provision. In all too many churches, nothing of the kind occurs, and the graduating student may be swiftly ordained and as swiftly immersed in his first charge.

Continuing Education

This is a point where we have much to learn from the other professions where the concept of 'continuing education' is rapidly gaining ground. Graduating doctors are required to complete a year or more of internship in a hospital, during which period they will be under strict educational supervision. And even when finally entered upon professional practice, the need for periodic refresher courses is increasingly recognized, as well of course as the need for further training before any form of specialization. So also for the engineer, and for the teacher—today's professional readily admits that his education had only begun when he left college, and that continued private study and periodic formal instruction are required if he is to keep abreast of later developments in professional knowledge and practice. In the ministry, such a notion is of very recent origin. Though in many churches there has been a tradition of private study and scholarship among the clergy, there have been few provisions for refresher courses or for systematic courses of study for younger ministers.

Today things are beginning to change. In Britain many churches are running schemes of post-ordination training for younger ministers. In France, Germany and Scandinavia, compulsory schemes for refresher or retraining courses exist for ministers who have served for five, or ten years in a parish. In the United States there are many such courses run by churches, seminaries and specialized institutions. Two national consultations on Continuing Education have built up a considerable body of experience on its aims, curricula and methods and have led to the formation of the Society for the Advancement of Continuing Education for Ministry (SACEM).[8] Though there is disagreement as to whether or not the theological school should bear primary responsibility for such courses there is agreement that the schools should prepare the students for continuing education and should not aim at turning out completely educated ministers. Further there is a clear advantage on both sides if many seminary staff are involved in the teaching of such courses. There is also agreement that the churches have responsibility to see that such continuing education takes place and that the ministers are able to profit from it. Either the denomination or the individual congregation must be prepared to take financial responsibility for the minister and for his family during such courses, and must see that he is not prevented from participating by reason of professional duties. Some churches are now thinking in terms of an annual or biennial period of several weeks continuing education in addition to a minister's regular vacation, and also of a longer period resembling a sabbatical year once or twice during his ministry.[9]

There is great variation in the kind of courses provided for the continuing education of the ministry. On the whole it seems that what is needed is not just academic study (though some ministers will profit from such studies and from a period of systematic reading). The aim of continuing education should not just be to catch up with younger contemporaries who have recently been at college. Certainly information and discussion on recent theological and non-theological thinking will normally find its place. But even more important is an opportunity to reflect together with others on the tasks of the ministry, and on the lessons which have already been learnt over the years in the performance of these tasks. One institution which exists for this specific purpose is the Institute of Advanced Pastoral Studies[10] near Detroit, which has helped many American ministers, after the first period of their ministry, to see what they are doing and how they are doing it, to relate the theology they learnt at seminary to the problems they have already met, and to rediscover the stance of the Christian minister in the world today. It is at this point perhaps, rather than earlier, that ministers begin to see what theological awareness, Christian presence and service for others, might really mean.

Another interesting example, this time from India, is the Tamilnad In-Service Training Project, an extension of the work of the Tamilnad Theological College, Tirumariayur. Here the director of the project has gone out to the dioceses where former students are at work and has gathered small groups of such ministers for a week's common study, discussion and prayer. He has followed up these conferences with visits by invitation to the pastorates of the men who have participated, spending three days in each of them with three aims in view:

a *Research* into the effectiveness of theological education;
b a *Teaching Mission* through which an attempt is made to bring before one selected congregation what it means to be 'the church of God in that place'; and

c *Fellowship*, in prayer and discussion, with men isolated from their ministerial colleagues.

In this example, the continuing education of ministers is combined with laity formation and with the evaluation of previous training, as an extension service of a theological school. In other parts of the world, notably in Latin America, where there are many pastors who have had only a minimal institutional training, similar extension programmes have been attempted as a substitute for institutional training. Both in Guatemala and in Chile, training teams using audio-visual material and programmed instruction take the education to the pastor, or to the layman with a call to the ministry, giving short courses in different centres all over the country. As C. Lalive d'Epinay points out in a recent article, this may be one of the few ways open to the main-line Protestant churches to make contact with the dynamic Pentecostal movement in Latin America.[11] It is interesting that the Christian Institute of South Africa is planning correspondence courses of programmed learning for pastors of the many African independent churches in southern Africa. Another instance of a structure of theological education 'in dispersion' would be the proposal for a first year of a theological course to be offered in a dozen or so different centres in East Africa, to be completed by a two-year course in the existing theological colleges.

10 · Planning the Curriculum

From the point of view of the student, most theological curricula have two disadvantages:

a there is too much to learn, and there is no clear relation between the different bits;

b no training is given for many of the tasks which ministers perform.

This situation leads to frustration and to the conviction that theological education is largely irrelevant. The inference is not unnatural, though we have seen that functional relevance does not demand the kind of direct and practical relationship which many students look for between what they learn at college and what they will have to do later on. What is important is that ministers should be ready and able to function in a variety of situations, and for this the functional orientation of the whole course is needed. But it is certainly true that theological curricula often appear to consist of discrete blocks of knowledge not clearly integrated with each other; and further, that theological schools might well offer some more specialized training for different patterns of ministry.

The Integrating Principle

Our main guide in drawing up a curriculum should be to *integrate* theory and practice. Integration is also necessary between the different parts of the traditional 'core'. The whole curriculum must be an organic unity; Church History and Systematics must not pull in different directions, any more than, for example, New Testament and Homiletics. This integration, which is required for practical and educational reasons is also theologically necessary. If we think of theology as a field of academic studies, containing several more or less independent disciplines, then there is no reason why these should not all pursue separate and presumably parallel paths. But if theology is 'exploration', if it demands existential commitment then we must think of it as a unity, which can only be expounded in an integrated way and in relation to our life in the world. It is noteworthy that this breakdown of traditional divisions is not peculiar to theology but is characteristic today of the natural and social sciences as well.

In planning a curriculum, our first question must then be to ask: What is the integrating principle? On the basis of our answer we can decide what to put into the curriculum and what to leave out, since all education must be selective, especially in these days of the 'information explosion', which has not left unmarked the field of theology. For the last twenty years or so, theological schools like other institutions of higher education, have been trying to cram more and more into their basic courses. Inevitably something has been left out, and no one has ever been happy about the omissions. Now it is time for theological education to decide on what principle the selection is to be made. This is another reason why continuing education is so important. If theological education is to stop when a student graduates, it must be as exhaustive as possible. If it is only the first stage of a continuing process, painting in the background, suggesting ways of organizing knowledge, teaching methods of understanding and practice—the pressure is not quite so great.

What then is the integrating principle to be? There are several possibilites. Traditionally it has been sought in the subject-matter of theology, in the biblical documents or the Christian tradition, the *depositum fidei*, with systematic theology as the central discipline. But this is a principle of comprehension rather than selection, which, if it excludes anything, would appear to exclude all that gives contemporary reference to the study of theology. It is against this view that the German students are rebelling, suggesting practical theology as a central discipline in place of systematics or the more popular hermeneutics. Practical theology they see as 'a science within the Church' which 'proves itself as a science by the methodical collection of information from the life of the church today and also by the considered transmission of theology and church'.[1]

This sentence may provide us with our clue. For the subject-matter of practical theology so defined is *the life and mission of the Church in the contemporary world.* It is here that the integrating principle is to be found: in the situation of the Church as the people of God seeking to perform God's will and to participate in his mission in the varied social and cultural contexts of the world today. The Christian tradition is not here forgotten, for the principle may be stated in terms of what one American seminary, introducing its new curriculum, names the 'Christian message—world polarity'; or what the former principal of an Asian seminary describes as the relation between 'Text and Context in Theological Education'.[2] The Church is what it is, because it has a message; its position in the world is problematic because of its need to be true to that message and to convey it to others.

This view has many advantages. It allows for flexibility: the situation of the Church changes, nor is it everywhere the same. It allows for objectivity: economists, sociologists and historians can bring their insights to bear upon it. It is based on Scripture: the history of salvation is concerned throughout with God's people in God's world. It demands existential involvement: it is in this situation that the Christian life has to be lived. It is an ecumenical starting-point: confessional distinctions do not here divide us. Finally it is related to the central task of the ministry, as we have defined it: the awareness, presence and service of Christians depend on their understanding of the Church's calling in the world today.

For this view there are many witnesses, notably in Asia and in eastern Europe. At the Hong Kong Consultation in 1965, for instance, the point was made by many speakers, and figures largely in the official Statement: 'It is our conviction that the theological school is at the heart of the task of renewing the Church for its ministry in mission'. And again, 'This new concern for society and culture does not mean a radical rejection of the traditional disciplines taught in a theological curriculum. It does, however, mean a radical rethinking of these disciplines, relating them to one another, to the ministry committed to the people of God, and to the world in which this ministry is to be exercised'.[3] And the Seoul Consultation the following year addressed eight questions to theological schools in North-East Asia of which the first is: 'Do courses of study consistently contain the dimension of mission?'[4] Further testimonies to the same point of view are contained in the special issue of the *International Review of Missions*, on 'Theological Education for Mission'; among them a very similar list of questions is put by a theological professor from the German Democratic Republic to his own church and seminary.[5] Commenting on these papers at the Northwood Consultation, a professor from Czechoslovakia maintained that, 'the crisis in theological education springs from the fact that the dimension is missing which could transcend church-interests and theological research and at the same time include both. We see this dimension in the truth of the Gospel which is ecumenical, and in which the whole creation shares. This truth can be understood only as mission—not as an introduction to running the church nor as a matter for theological research . . . Specialization in theological education should be balanced by an integrating factor. We see this integrating factor as the mission of the Church to lead the struggle for man and his future.'[6]

The word 'mission' in all these quotations is to be understood in a broad sense as referring primarily to the work of God who is seeking to unify all things and all persons in Christ. This concept of the *Missio Dei* has been introduced recently into ecumenical thinking and was a subject of lively debate at the Fourth Assembly of the World Council of Churches.[7] It is widely held that old notions of mission need to be revised, but the concept itself is intrinsic to the essence of the Church, and should therefore be our 'organizing principle' in planning theological education.

In this connection it is interesting to remember that in the report which Keith Bridston prepared in 1954 for the World's Student Christian Federation, as a precursor of the present ecumenical study, he suggested that the 'unifying centre for theological training' might be found in what he termed *ecumenism*, namely 'the unity and mission of the Church'.[8] If ecumenism is understood in this way as concerned as much with the mission and renewal of the Church as with its unity, we may accept this judgement. To say this, however, is not to affirm that missiology or ecumenics as currently taught should form the centre of the theological curriculum. The curriculum must be recast in an ecumenical and missionary dimension.

Towards an Integrated Curriculum

How is this to be done? If we accept as our integrating principle the life and mission of the Church in the contemporary world, what are the implications for the planning of the theological curriculum? What selection shall we make from the material that might be included? What teaching methods should we employ? In what follows, we shall consider six possible implications, before going on, in the last part of the chapter, to discuss the question of specialization.

1. The integrating principle can help us to select an *overall theme* to serve as an introduction to theological studies. Thus in Tainan Theological College, Taiwan, the first year starts with a course on 'The Gospel, the World and the Ministry', to be followed in the second semester by parallel courses on 'The People of God in Formosa Today' and 'The People of God in the Old Testament'. In the United Theological Seminary of the Twin Cities in the USA, the Bachelor of Divinity curriculum begins with three closely related courses on: 'The Christian Faith and the Social Order', 'The Church's Ministry of Preaching and Worship', and 'The Constructive Task of Theology'. The German *Fakultätentag* recommends that at the beginning of the theological course two introductory series of lectures should be given on 'The Whole Field of Theology' and on 'The Life and Work of the Church'.

Other American seminaries take a somewhat different emphasis, starting from the situation of the student as personally involved in the cultural and institutional crisis of the West today. Thus Chicago Divinity School accepts the 'problematic character of theological statements' and the consequent need for the theological student (professional or lay) to discover for himself the 'style' of an authentic ministry. Not a hundred yards from the seminar room where Divinity School students meet weekly for a seminar on 'The Ministry of the Church in Contemporary Society', Chicago Theological Seminary begins its Bachelor of Divinity syllabus with an intensive four-week course on 'Christian Existence', directed at the personal cultivation of theological awareness. There are of course many other possibilities. The important point is that in all of them an attempt is made to give a general introduction to the whole course, either by starting with the known situation of the Church today, or by portraying the main lines of God's action in history. The relevance of what comes later is thus easily seen, and the student perceives at the beginning where the curriculum as a whole is going.[9]

2. Different subjects can be taught *in relation to each other* and attention directed to the connections between them. Experiments in 'team-teaching' have been introduced from medical education and other fields. Two theological teachers belonging to different disciplines can together teach a particular course, stressing the interrelation of systematics and ethics, for instance, or of biblical and historical theology. This method has also been used effectively to bridge the gap between the 'classical' and the 'practical' subjects. In certain American seminaries, students have been assigned to particular field projects together with a professor from one of the classical disciplines, whose task it is to go with them to the hospital or urban centre and to help them reflect on the relevance of theological insights to their group experience. The two-year experiment of Boston University School of Theology in 1961-1963 in 'A New Combination of Clinical, Academic and Parish Training' should also

be cited, though this presupposed basic theological education, and concentrated on the relation of practical work to the development of a 'Theology of the Parish'.

3. The *method of presentation* of certain subjects should certainly be changed. This is particularly true in the historical field. Peter G. Gowing has suggested how a relevant Church history might be taught in an African or Asian setting, and H. J. Margull has outlined a programme for teaching mission in a Japanese seminary starting from a world in rapid social change and ending with futurology. In systematic theology and in ethics the case-study method has been used with effect. As we have seen, Keith Bridston developed this in Indonesia, where he found that students were not very interested in the implications of the Chalcedonian controversy, but were 'vitally concerned with the theological implications of the ideological debates swirling about Sukarno and other political leaders'. In its recent thinking the Theological Education Fund has devoted much attention to relating the teaching of theology to the dialectic between the renaissance of local cultures and the increasingly universal technological civilization. Studies have also been made on teaching particular subjects such as biblical theology in Asia or in Africa.[10]

4. As a more general point, we may note the advantages of using an *inductive method* in theological teaching. In recent educational theory attention has been focused on how students learn, and two kinds of learning distinguished:

a the learning of subject-matter which is facilitated by a structural approach, which from the start enables students to organize information in a meaningful way; and

b the learning how to learn which builds on the particular skills and knowledge of individual students.

The case-study method will help with the first of these, as will also, for instance, the device used by Professor William Hamilton in his first-year theology course at Colgate-Rochester, when he asks students to keep a theological journal, noting down each day an event they have experienced and attempting to reflect on its theological significance. The second kind of learning takes place in supervised field education and also in mixed theoretical and practical courses such as that on 'Human Growth and Development' proposed by a working party of the British Council of Churches on the lines of courses undertaken by students of social work. In the Church of England a course is now under way at Lichfield Theological College designed primarily for students who have difficulty with the normal academic approach, and constructed on the 'sandwich-method' with alternate periods of practical experience (in industry and elsewhere) and of study in college where reflection on that experience is used as the jumping-off place for theological instruction.[11]

5. In discussing *supervision* C. R. Feilding points out that this is also applicable to academic work. It can indeed be connected with the function of the tutorial in the ancient English universities (though in other circumstances a tutorial may mean a seminar). He does not develop this point at length and readers are left to transpose for themselves to other settings the concept of supervision described in the chapter by Thomas Klink. But some interesting experiments in theological education depend on making just this transposition. The programme at Lichfield mentioned above assumes that students will be under supervision both in college and out of it. In St. Paul's School of Theology, Kansas City, second-year students spend their whole time in 'functional units' dealing with particular aspects of the Church's task under the supervision of two faculty-members, one from the theological and one from the practical field. Again the proposals of the *Fakultätentag* call for the introduction of 'supervision' (*Kontrolle*) in German universities in the first few semesters after passing the language exams.

It is also important that careful attention should be given to the use of the small group as an instrument of formal education; its more general educational value will be discussed in the next chapter.

One interesting example is that of Salisbury Theological College where students receive an induction course on learning-method, including sensitivity training, when they enter the college, and teams of students under supervision form an integral part of the academic programme as well as these units for field education and for the arrangement of worship.[12]

6. Finally we must consider the place of the *biblical languages*. Earlier discussion on the reformation of theological studies tended to conclude that this was a place where economies were possible, and many churches ceased to require their ministers to study Hebrew, or even Greek. Recent interest in Old Testament theology questions this conclusion. Theological schools in Asia and Africa today are beginning to teach Greek and Hebrew through the medium of the local vernacular. Though the study of the ancient languages cannot be made compulsory for all ministers, most theological schools now feel that provision should be made for those students who wish to do so to study them, and those with linguistic ability should be encouraged to do this.

A recent report commissioned by the AATS asserts strongly that the study of the biblical languages is even more necessary today than it seemed to be in the past. More efficient and imaginative programmes of language study are necessary, such as the crash-courses now given in some schools, or the alternative courses introducing the structure and key concepts of the biblical languages for those who are not intending to specialize in them. There is room for more research and experiment here in the preparation of instruction material and the use of teaching aids, but also in the kind of skills required by students for an understanding of Scripture in the original tongues. The report suggests for instance that the specialized skill of translating is not required by most students today in view of the many modern Bible translations that exist.[13]

Specialization

If the curriculum is not to be too heavy a certain amount of speciali-

zation will be required. This is particularly true if a more diversified concept of the ministry is adopted. Specialist ministers require
specialized training, though much of this can be at the post-graduate
level. Karl Rahner, among others, has recommended that 'the identification between the training of a pastoral priest and of a scholarly
theological must be abolished'. [14] Theological education has too long
trained men for the ministry by submitting them to a scientific education designed primarily for future scholars. What is needed, Rahner
suggests, is a new kind of theology for pastors with an 'unambig-
uously pastoral orientation', and many would agree with him.

Recently, there have been some developments in this direction,
notably in Germany where the *Fakultätentag* recommends two alternative courses, after the completion of the first exam (which 'should
be capable of attainment by the students of average ability within
the time stated'). While the intending pastor would serve as a *Vikar*
(or probationer minister) and attend a *Predigerseminar* (or Pastoral
Institute) as formerly, the 'academically gifted' student would have
the possibility of post-graduate studies leading eventually to a
doctoral degree. In the States, on the other hand, some seminaries
are now developing doctorates designed for professional ministers.
Thus at Chicago Divinity School the Bachelor of Divinity degree has
been replaced by a combined degree of Master of Theology and
Doctor of Ministry. The future theologian will not take either
degree but will work instead for the research-oriented Master of
Arts and Doctor of Philosophy programme.

This dichotomy is no doubt desirable, but leaving aside the
rather special needs of the future scholar or theological teacher, is not
a far greater degree of diversification required? Do not the specialized
ministries, described in Part I of this book, or even the different
patterns of pastoral ministry appropriate in different areas, each
require a particular course of training, with a different balance of
components? Should theological schools not follow the example of
Yale Divinity School which for many years now has required its
students to specialize in one of five courses leading to different church

vocations, namely pastoral ministry, campus Christian leadership, religious education, missions, college teaching or research?

If we take seriously the suggestion made by Canon J. V. Taylor that five different categories of ministers should replace our existing clergy, then each category might require a different kind of training. Taylor himself suggests that they should all receive a basic training, together with the laity 'on a quite local level, related to a single area and to a particular local community'—much of it through part-time courses. Specialized training would follow, and would take place in institutions corresponding to our present theological colleges.[15]

On the whole, however, it seems wise to resist too early a specialization and this for two reasons. We have insisted on the need for ministers to be ready for anything, to be prepared to think theologically and to act as Christians in entirely new situations for which they have not been trained. Specialized knowledge and skill must be developed wherever possible, but often at a much later stage, and the basic attitudes and skill requred are the same in every situation. Again we have stressed the need for partnership, the need for ministers to work in teams. Here too it is important that the different members of a team ministry should be equipped as far as possible for any specific functions they have to fulfil, but the prior requirement is to be able to work with others whose knowledge and skills are different. A common basic theological education is therefore important—and indeed it is desirable that part of this should be shared by the lay specialists as well. And so the development of post-graduate institutions specializing in different kinds of ministry seems the wisest course. It is this kind of specialization which is recommended in the AATS proposals. In Europe, too, it has been suggested that certain faculties should specialize in post-graduate courses for army chaplains, for ministers in industry and for those in radio and TV.

11 · Learning in Community

There is one aspect of theological education which figures in all discussions of the subject: the current uncertainty regarding traditional patterns of devotional or spiritual formation. These have been conceived in the past, both by Catholics and by Protestants, primarily in terms of the individual minister. Today we are beginning to see that the real lack is one of community formation. It is not the individual spiritual discipline, whether nourished on the Bible or on liturgical offices, that is chiefly lacking, but the experience of being moulded by the Spirit into a Christian fellowship where each supplies the deficiencies of his fellows and where all together can form an instrument more or less adequate for the Lord's service. If the minister is to serve as the focus of a Christian community, he must know what Christian community can mean, and must learn to use the resources of Scripture, prayer and liturgy within such a community.[1]

In discussing this subject, attention must therefore be directed to the whole question of community in the theological school. For residential colleges this is an obvious problem, even if only on the practical level; participation in a Christian community has always been one of their aims. In higher education generally today, the question of community life baulks larger than previously. It is no longer respectable to praise the nine-to-five university where students gather to listen to lectures but for no other purpose. Yet much higher education, and much theological education too, still takes this form. We are much more conscious today of the need of the individual for a community to which he can belong, and also of the educational opportunities a community of students can afford.

Theological schools can no longer be divided into those where community matters and those where it is irrelevant—a division roughly corresponding to the Catholic-Protestant divide. The division still persists, but the two groups would now be better characterized as

a those schools which hang on to a traditional conception of community life though increasingly doubtful of its relevance to the modern age, and
b those schools without a community structure which do not know where to find one.

Perhaps this is harsh, but for the church-related school it is the number one problem. Universities tend to see it differently as part of a larger problem even less easy to resolve. At a conference of British theological college principals in Birmingham, some years ago, it was interesting to see how the Free Church colleges looked to the Anglican ones for leading here and were surprised to discover that they felt themselves equally at sea.

The traditional justification of the seminary in the Roman Catholic Church has not, as a matter of fact, rested upon a particularly developed view of community life. The model was the cloister, and the significant symbol the perimeter wall which kept the world out, rather than the common hall where students ate and might talk together. The aim has been personal perfection rather than the development of a model Christian community. Certainly there has been discipline, a common way of life, participation in the Church's worship, and professional supervision as described above. All these are advantages the 'Protestant' school has often lacked, and as Bridston indicates, they have provided an ideological and a spiritual formation perfectly functional for traditional views of the priesthood. But now in the Roman Church, as in other churches which have shared in part the seminary tradition, the function of the priest is less clear, and the traditional training is less appropriate. If the Christian community is primary then a different kind of community life may well be required in the seminary.[2]

The Northwood Consultation, as indeed the others which preceded it, gave much attention to this question, and the Recommendations which it made were carefully worded. *Recommendation 27*[3] deserves closer examination. Theology, it says, involved *dialogue*; and so community is important. We cannot learn theology alone any more than we can learn alone the other disciplines of the university. The basic structure of education must be collegiate, and this is as true of theology as of the other humane disciplines. Nor can the dialogue be an in-group dialogue. This we have seen already. The implication here is that theological learning occurs where students are in dialogue with others in meaningful groups, which are not divorced from the larger community, but share in its nature. An earlier attempt at formulating this truth reads as follows: 'It must not be thought that learning in community is confined to closely-knit committed groups. Indeed, one of our present needs is that Christians should learn to live among groups of other allegiance and loosely federated, ever-changing associations. At the university, dedication to the pursuit of learning promotes a partnership between teachers and students in common exploration and research which creates a community based on mutual responsibility and trust.'[4]

Not all university education is of this character; it is unrealistic to look at a modern university only in this way. But it is still true that theological education takes this aspect of community less seriously than it should. We should therefore welcome such changes in university structure as make this easier, as well as such student initiatives as the spontaneous student-led seminar emerging in some countries today. Again we should welcome the AATS proposals described in Chapter 9, which include at Level II, in the theological 'nucleus', a problem-centred seminar using the inductive method and consisting of ten to twelve students with a staff-member as resource-person. Students will spend a quarter of their time in this 'core' programme (contrast the usual use of the word in theological education to refer to systematic instruction in the four classical disciplines). The groups are intended to be the basis of community life and of worship and to 'represent the involvement of all members in a common effort to understand and to act responsibly in the modern world'.[5]

Theology is also 'an *existential* enterprise' in which the student is challenged to commit himself to the Christian faith. It is not just the faith of his teachers that challenges him, as if he were the disciple of an esoteric philosophy. It is the faith of the community, a community in which he was probably brought up, a community which encounters him in his teachers and in his fellow students, a community struggling to express its faith in intelligible terms for today. Often, though not always, he is already committed to Christian belief. Yet as he examines it for the first time critically and with scientific tools he will need the faith of the community around him if his own faith is to grow in maturity. 'Ideological crystallization' cannot take place in a vacuum. It never has, of course; in those traditions where the community aspect of theological education has not been emphasized, the student has often been supported by some other community—it may be his local congregation, the Student Christian Movement or some other group. Yet in so far as the university or theological college has not itself been a community, the student's task has certainly been made more difficult. If theological teachers and students have not seemed to rejoice in the freedom of their 'life together' (as Bonhoeffer terms it) the seriousness of the Gospel has been called in question. The formal side of theological education has remained uninfluenced by the substance.

So much for the need for community, what then of its character? The last sentence of *Recommendation* 27 reads as follows: the student 'must be given *freedom* to discover his own identity as a Christian and his place in the Church, by learning to use the tools of knowledge and the *tradition and wisdom of the community* under the guidance of a teacher and *together with his peers.*'

The theological community must be *free*. The theological student is not a conscript, nor is he a child. He has freely entered on his studies. The discipline—and there must be discipline—must not be imposed but freely accepted. Only so can he discover what it means to be Christian in Luther's terms, as 'the most free Lord of all and subject to none'; only so can he discover his place in the free community of the Church in which he is 'the most dutiful servant of all and subject to every one'. Theological students are adults; it is dangerous to treat them as children. Spiritual formation is not assisted by the petty requirements of a boarding school—to be found in Protestant theological colleges as much as Roman Catholic ones. Where the students themselves have some say in the nature of the common discipline, it is both more effective and more fruitful.

Freedom of this kind characterizes the life of the Protestant Faculty at Montpellier, which Professor Créspy described at the Northwood Consultation, where students participate in weekly faculty meetings, and where full meetings of the community took place regularly during the Algerian war so that all members could express themselves freely on their political views. Créspy comments, 'Students find their prolonged adolescence and the deferment of responsibility to the future extremely difficult. They seek compensation, which is usually intellectual. Their desire for involvement is expressed in the community which becomes a microcosm of the city or of the church, without necessarily having any direction or meaning. What is the remedy? . . . Spiritual problems are problems of relationships. Therefore, a theological community is bound to reveal problems; the community is therapeutic . . . Can there be such a thing as a spiritually balanced community? Perhaps not—though it *may* be balanced if the leaders are balanced. Theological teachers have an unwritten responsibility to be balanced persons and this balance is not achieved by study!'[6]

And so, the *tradition and wisdom of the community* have an important place. Theological education requires a teacher, and of the teacher much is demanded. If he is to be a true educator his responsibility and his influence cannot be limited to the class-room. Nor can the teacher operate alone; he too must be subject to the community.

Patterns of Ministry

The wisdom and authority of the community do not necessarily reside in the senior member, either in terms of age or position. All Christian communities are microcosms of the whole Church; our view of the ministry must therefore apply also to the ministry of the theological teacher and the college principal. It is Christ within the community who is the Minister. All members of the community, students as well as teachers, bring the gifts of ministry which they have received and which require to be developed. All must work together in partnership.

So finally the student learns *together with his peers*. It is the peer-group which is the primary educational influence. This insight, familiar in educational theory, has been prominent in the development of Clinical Pastoral Education and in the concept of supervision described in an earlier chapter. It has also been the discovery of Roman Catholic seminaries which have introduced the team or *équipe* as the unit of seminary life. Where this development has taken place, students have been prepared, as by no other method, to take their place later on in ministerial teams. Traditional methods of theological education, both Catholic and Protestant, have trained ministers to work independently from each other. If ministers are to work in teams they must be trained in teams.

The Value of Teams

As indicated above, the team-concept in theological education was first developed in the *Mission de France*, which was essentially concerned with training priests to work in missionary teams. It is the ecclesial nature of the team that guarantees the apostolic character of its presence in the world. On entering the seminary students are divided into teams of five or six members. There is a priest in each team, but he is not the team-leader, and the teachers at the seminary themselves form a team which is subject to the same discipline. The teams are units of practical work, but they are also spiritual and pastoral communities. The faith of their members is sustained by mutual examination of conscience (*revision de vie*) in full fraternal communion with other members of the team.

In other Roman Catholic seminaries, in France, Belgium and Holland, and in the United States, there is a further development, and the teams become units both of academic work and of missionary involvement. In some cases, as at Louvain and in Amsterdam, the seminarians live in teams, in separate houses or apartments together with a priest.[7] This also happens at the Church of England colleges, at Wells and Salisbury.

In *The Seminary: Protestant and Catholic*, Walter D. Wagoner describes two Belgian seminaries which use the team-method and comments that such experiments 'are encouraging re-definitions of the older Catholic concept of spirituality; the intention now is to involve the student in the world of the laity, to correlate prayer and action, to make curriculum more relevant, to treat the student as a mature person and to increase faculty-student rapport'.

Though recognizing that the background and the problems of the Protestant seminary are different, Wagoner maintains that similar re-definitions are there required. The phrases 'spirituality' and 'spiritual formation' tend indeed to suggest a dichotomy between spiritual and material things which most Protestants and many Catholics would want to reject. Yet he believes that the time has now come for Protestants to learn from 'the Catholic vision and experience of the spiritual life' doing violence to 'Protestant theological integrity' and for Catholics to learn from Protestants at 'a moment of expanding ecumenicity'. 'In the realm of spiritual and devotional life', he comments, 'it may be much easier to modify the Catholic tradition than to reinvigorate the Protestant.'[8] Many would disagree with this judgement; and it might be nearer the truth to admit that neither tradition can hope to survive alone unscathed the current questioning of the concept and patterns of spirituality.

This questioning first came into the light of day when, in *Honest to God*, an Anglican bishop confessed the bankruptcy from his point of view of the traditional spirituality inculcated at his theological college and pleaded for a pattern of prayer based not on disengagement but on engagement.[9] Much of this questioning has been negative, and much, of positive value, has been misunderstood. There are some signs now that a more constructive period is beginning. The speakers at the 1967 Parish and People Conference in England on 'Spirituality Today' were prepared to affirm the value of traditional teaching and, at the same time, the urgent need for its reinterpretation and re-formulation. The conference chairman, Dean Coburn of the Episcopal Theological School at Cambridge, Massachusetts, who was also chairman of the US Study Group on Patterns of Ministry and Theological Education, in a paper entitled 'The New Mood in Spirituality', accepts Robinson's contention that prayer is worked through in engagement, but stresses the need of disengagement as well. He is well aware that for contemporary theological students the *Exercises of St. Ignatius* have been supplanted by Michael Quoist's *Prayers of Life*[10] as devotional material, and is glad of the change.

In another of the conference papers, John Townroe welcomes Quoist's book as a sign of 'a new Christian spirituality emerging today'. He points to the significant fact 'that *Prayers of Life* was not written by one man alone, nor by a priest alone' but stemmed from a group of committed Christians. 'Surely', he says, 'this is how you should expect a genuinely contemporary spirituality to appear. Such a thing cannot be manufactured to order. It needs to grow from life'. And John Coburn says the same.[11]

Development of Community Life

If this is true, it would seem that spiritual formation should not be thought of as something distinct from the other aspects of theological education, nor the spiritual formation of the clergy as different in kind from that which laymen also require. As the Northwood Recommendations put it, 'the committed Christian who is *not* ordained . . . is right to expect theology to be related to the mission and life of the Church as well as to contemporary society; and he will hope to receive some spiritual formation by participation in a committed community'. It is through this participation, this 'learning in community', that spiritual formation takes place, and not primarily through the study of ascetical theology or through schooling in the traditional methods of prayer—though these have their place. The weakness of spiritual formation, which is widely acknowledged today, derives therefore to a large extent from defects in community. The institution of teams, as units of community life, will go part of the way to remedy some of these defects. But there are others and to these we must briefly turn in concluding this chapter.

1. The community of a theological school is a real community, for better or for worse, it is not just a place where community may be practised. It is of course an unbalanced community, and to some extent a segregated one, but it is important that students and staff-members alike should take seriously their membership of this community, however temporary, and that the community itself should take seriously its relation to society, and to the Church. The example of Montpellier, quoted above, shows how a theological school can become intellectually involved in the problems of society. Intellectual involvement in the problems of the Church is more common, though it does not take place automatically, since the intellectual concerns of the theological school may be unrelated to the problems with which the Church is concerned. Practical involvement is also possible and although it should not be taken to excess, there is a prima facie obligation on the theological school to consider where and how far it should occur.

The Statement of the Hong Kong Consultation on Theological Education in South-East Asia, 1965, referred to these obligations:

'The theological school must pay more attention', it said, 'to understanding its own role as a community dedicated to the one ministry entrusted to the Church in Christ, with its own special task of theological education'. It described this role in four ways:

a as 'the intellectual centre of the Church';

b as 'a vital worshipping community';

c as 'a witnessing community, deeply involved in the world', and especially in the immediate environs of the school campus;

d as 'a laboratory for the Church', an experimental station for the development of 'new patterns of worship, indigenous music, visual arts, new symbols, new forms of architecture, drama and creative writing in keeping with basic Christian faith, and the new social context of many countries and cultures'.[12]

Many of the schools represented at that Consultation are deeply involved in social and welfare projects, in agricultural development, in artistic and liturgical experiment and in the ongoing work of evangelism and pastoral care in the wider community.[13] Clearly these projects have considerable educational value for those who participate in them, but they should also be seen as ways in which the community can discharge its responsibility for the larger world of which it is part.

2. The community of the theological school should be a worshipping community, but a worshipping community of a certain kind. As suggested above, it has a peculiar opportunity for developing 'new patterns of worship'; it can be a centre of liturgical and also of ecumenical experiment. This is particularly the case where students from different churches study together; and it should be seen as one of the advantages of the united school. Where denominational colleges are linked or federated, it is surely best to have a common chapel and a common-worship life however varied. Indeed there is no better way of ensuring the richness and vitality of the Church's worship in the future—I would want to add a richness and vitality that comes from merging separate traditions—than that of

allowing ministers while they are students to experiment in developing forms of worship which are meaningful to themselves and significant to others because they arise from the thinking and involvement of that particular community. Such worship will provide the necessary context for a spiritual formation today far better than the continued and unchanging repetition of worship-forms devised for another century and for other circumstances.

3. The community of the theological schools tends, as we have said, to be an unbalanced community, but the imbalance is often artificially increased. Though in some churches the monastery still provides a valid model for the theological seminary, we have seen that even in the Roman Catholic Church this is being questioned today. Churches in which a married clergy is commoner than a celibate one, or in which women are admitted to some or to all forms of the ministry, may be creating unnecessary problems by continuing to assume that the celibate single-sex residential community is and must remain the norm. Theological schools in England and Germany have tended to ignore the fact that many students are married and have exiled wives and families to a 'decent' distance. If this distorts the community, it distorts still more the doctrine of Christian marriage; and it does not provide an adequate preparation for a married ministry in a mixed and open community.

Today, however, things are changing. The Lutheran Church of Hanover has built a *Predigerseminar* for married couples. Several Church of England colleges now welcome wives to live in college housing or nearby and to take some part in the college community. In one of them 'wives and sweethearts' vote in college conferences and share in practical groups, and once a week college worship is a family affair with women and children taking a leading part. In some African schools students are encouraged to come with their wives and families to live in a student village, because of the opportunity thereby given for the practical education of students' wives and for establishing the model of a Christian home.

Some American seminaries have made a determined effort not only to provide housing for married couples but to integrate the wives and children of students into the community, a community which consists of men and women, married and unmarried, teachers and students, from different churches and backgrounds, and it may be also from different countries, and which may also include those who are not training for the Christian ministry. There is clearly much to be gained from a mixed community of this kind, though it can perhaps only be realized if the school is of a certain size.

The provision of residential accommodation may not of course always be the solution; a prior need, as Wagoner points out, is for the development of new community patterns for married communities. 'The American Protestant seminaries', he says, 'have been so busy for the last ten years simply trying to provide the new housing facilities, jobs, etc. for this married population that the spiritual formation (of married communities) has been neglected. This is obviously a major problem, and it ought to be the subject of special research.'

Nor is it simply a question of married students. Since many churches now ordain women, women students take their places beside the men in their own right. Community formation in the theological school cannot assume a single-sex community. The development of new patterns at this point will therefore have a wider application than before since the situation more closely resembles that of the Christian congregation. Here, too, the wholeness of theological education is seen. Patterns of community life developed in the theological school may also apply to the local Christian community, and the spiritual formation of laymen may be seen as continuous with that of ministers.

12 · Theological Education for the Whole People of God

'The aim of theological education cannot be limited to the training of students for professional ministry, as pastors or theologians, in a particular church. It should rather be the education of all Christians for a diversified ministry within a united Church. This diversified ministry would indeed include a wide range of specialized ministries for which a degree of professional training is required. But it would also include the still wider range of lay witness and service in a variety of professional, social and cultural contexts, as well as in the domestic life of the Christian congregation.'

This paragraph from an interim report of the Study on Patterns of Ministry and Theological Education[1] summarizes the theme of this book. In the first part we have tried to spell out at greater length what a diversified ministry might mean within the greater diversity of witness and service which is God's gift to his Church. In the second part we have concentrated on the professional training which some Christians must continue to receive, but always within the context of a wider view of theological education. Now we must try and state what in fact this wider view should imply for the education of Christians who are not preparing for a professional ministry.

We have already noted in Chapter 6 three basic implications stressed by the Northwood Consultation. The first of these is obvious, but it is also extremely important, and it formed in fact the first recommendation of the Consultation: that *programmes of theological education for 'the ministry' and for 'the laity' should be fully co-ordinated*. In most churches this is not the case at present; different boards and agencies are responsible, in most cases, for ministerial training and for laity formation.[2] Very often there is little co-ordination between these different boards. Almost inevitably, the larger resources, both in institutions and manpower, in endowments and annual budget, are deployed by the board responsible for the theological education of the clergy. It is usually regarded as an axiom that the training of the clergy has prior claim on the funds of the Church, and that laity formation, together with other additional programmes (including for instance the continuing education of the clergy), can only expect a share of the residue once this claim has been fully discharged.

Certainly the training of the clergy is an important—and an expensive—item, but it is doubtful whether it should always remain a prior charge on the resources of the churches. In the sixteenth century the Reformation churches stressed the need for educating the whole people of God, partly indeed because only an educated church can produce an educated clergy, but also because they esteemed that a certain degree of education was required for a mature Christian. Although much effort and great resources are put into the work of Christian education today, this is still thought of as a secondary enterprise, and as part of the work of the clergy. And besides, the emphasis tends to be on the Christian education of children, whether in the congregation or in the church school, and the education of mature Christian laymen becomes a separate (and junior) enterprise, under the name of lay training or laity formation.

All these aspects of education are surely part of one whole. They need to be co-ordinated; they need to be planned together. It is highly desirable that they be put on one budget, so that the churches can decide responsibly where, in a given situation and at a given time, the most money is needed and the best teachers required. Such a joint enterprise would make it possible for buildings to be used now in one way and now in another, and sometimes, perhaps, in several ways at the same time. Some churches are already discussing this possibility.[3]

Laymen at Theological Schools

The *second* implication is the need for courses of theological education to be shared by future ministers and laymen. We have noted
two tendencies in theological schools today: On the one hand,
there is the increase of students entering such schools without
specific vocational commitment; and on the other, there is the
broadening of theological courses away from a narrow professional
orientation. On the whole, theological educators have welcomed
these tendencies. Should they now go the further step of stating
explicitly that as many laymen as can and as wish to do so should
study theology at theological schools? This would complete
the transformation of these schools from seminaries for future
pastors and theologians, into training centres for the whole
Church.

There are different views on this issue. Though many theological
educators would welcome such a step, some would maintain that the
pastor and the layman require a different kind of training and that
the two functions should therefore be kept separate. Interestingly
enough at least one of the respondents to the questionnaire of the
Theological Education Fund, mentioned in Chapter 6, has recently
changed his mind on this question. Some years ago, when involved
in planning a theological course, he felt that it should be limited to
ordinands but 'I have now come to think', he writes, 'that the
highest priority must be given to the development of the type of
ordained ministry which really works to create a fully activated
laity, and consequently I now believe that clergy training should not
be separated from that of those who do not intend to offer for
ordination.' The Northwood Consultation, as a whole, agreed with
him, maintaining that 'shared courses should be the rule' but that
'even where courses are distinct, there is no reason why ministerial
education should always take place in separate institutions from
which lay persons are totally excluded.'[4]

What form such courses should take was not fully discussed by
the Northwood Consultation which had neither the time nor the

experience to consider the problems involved. A consultation in Bangalore, India, in April 1968 discussed the topic.[5] The participants welcomed the conclusions of the Northwood Consultation and reiterated many of them in their own finding. Thus, in the section which relates to courses for lay people at theological colleges, they develop a curriculum including study in three areas: (a) the contemporary world, (b) the Christian tradition, and (c) learning to live as persons. They stress that the three areas should be related to each other, that 'the layman should be taught to live and think theologically in a particular immediate context'. They see the programme as including 'deliberate exposure of the student to his secular environment and ... direct confrontation to significant current events'. They stress, further, the need to share in the common life of the college community, asserting that 'theology can be learnt only in fellowship'. All these points, made with courses for laymen in mind, apply just as much, as we have seen, to courses for future pastors. The kind of education described is in fact the same and might, in many cases, be shared.

In outlining this programme, the Bangalore consultation noted certain basic problems. There is the danger of divorcing formal education from everyday experience; the course described above seeks to avoid this with its stress on the context and on the environment. There is the difficulty of creating the right motivation; this they propose to do by describing the course from the students' perspective so that it is seen as helping in the realization of a fuller life.

There is, further, the variety of persons who offer themselves for theological training for one motive or another. In addition to those with professional motivation (future pastors and lay church-workers) there are five groups seeking theological education to whom it 'gives no direct economic advantage'. These are: (a) Christian teachers, some of them in church schools and with responsibility for Christian religious teaching, (b) government officers, (c) members of other professions, (d) those engaged in industry, and (e) housewives. The course described above is aimed at all these groups; it assumes possession of a college degree; it does not assume church-membership—'while our aim is the preparation of Christians for their part in the mission of the Church in the world, men of other faiths would not be excluded'. What is envisaged is either (a) a one-year course at an existing theological college, or (b) directed private study for most of the year including field investigation and analysis, followed by a concentrated six-week programme either at the college or at a temporary local centre. There is also a need for courses which would not require the same academic qualifications and which would be conducted by a church or group of churches, with a college faculty sharing in the preparation, and perhaps also in the teaching, through visits of teams to local centres.

Courses of this kind are already being run in many theological schools throughout the world.[6] The Indian proposals are particularly interesting because they relate to an area where Christianity is a minority religion, where theological instruction is not available in secular institutions, and where the number of Christians with the academic qualification required for a formal theological course is fairly low. Even in this situation there are many Christians with a certain standard of general education who would like to take a theological course in spite of the fact that they do not need it for professional reasons. A number of possible programmes are suggested for laymen in different circumstances and with different educational standards. Clearly a far greater variety of programmes would be needed, and they would have to be worked out in far greater detail, if the Church in India is to become a fully educated church.

This is not only true of India. It is equally true in other areas, including Europe and North America. We can now see that in addition to the false assumption that only professional ministers need theological education two other assumptions have been generally but wrongly made: (1) that there is only one kind of theological education, (2) that it can only be conducted on one level. Variety of courses and of standards has indeed existed, but it has not been welcomed. So long as theology is thought of as a body of knowledge which must be transmitted in propositional form, the highest academic standards and a basically academic programme have seemed to be essential. Without disputing the need for a high standard and for an academic approach for those that can profit from it, we may now hold that many Christians can learn to think theologically in different ways and at a different level.

The Study on Patterns of Ministry and Theological Education has been primarily concerned with the training of professional ministers, though at an early stage it was seen that the subject could not finally be limited in this way.[7] Neither can it be limited to the kind of courses which may appropriately be taught in existing institutions even when these are thrown open to laymen. So we come to a *third* implication of our approach to theological education: *If the whole people of God is to receive some sort of theological education, then the structure and institutions of theological education we have today must be changed beyond recognition.* It is ridiculous to suppose that every adult Christian, even if he had the time, could profit from the kind of course which theological schools at present give. A far greater variety of courses and institutions will be required.

In discussing theological education for laymen we should by no means confine ourselves to those who can profit from a university course or from a post-graduate course at a theological college. While I believe that we should encourage all Christians who proceed to university for higher education or to some other institute for professional training, to devote some time to the study of theology either at university or afterwards at a comparable level, this should not be our only thrust or indeed our main one. The number of university courses in theology is increasing, as is the number of students taking them, but a ceiling will certainly be reached. What is primarily needed is the organization of theological courses at a lower level, in a variety of centres and with maximum flexibility of programme and methodology.

A Utopian Proposal

The Bangalore Consultation started with the actual or potential resources available in India for lay theological education. This is the realistic starting-point, and it is similar to the one which we have taken throughout this study. But suppose that we start from the other end. Sometimes in planning it is useful to begin with the kind of situation you believe to be desirable, even though it is not certain how you can get there. Such a plan cannot be a blueprint. To some extent it must be Utopian, but it is necessary all the same if our blueprints are to be adequate. Inevitably the outlines must be vague. One reason for this is that such a plan, if it is to be workable, must take as much account as possible of the variation of circumstances from place to place. A plan of this kind is developed in the paragraphs that follow. It is not intended to be normative but to provoke discussion in an area where new research is needed.

We shall begin with the principle stated in Chapter 6. Theological education is a whole. The churches have a responsibility for the education of all their members parallel to their responsibility for proclamation, worship and service—and closely related to them. This responsibility cannot fully be discharged at the congregational level, whether through Sunday schools, catechism classes and youth groups or through the use of the pulpit for the systematic teaching of Christian doctrine. A continuing programme of adult education is also required (whether it be termed 'theological' education or not) and this cannot adequately be done by each congregation for itself. The primary aim of such adult education is not to impart information, nor to inculcate appropriate response in a passive laity, but to involve the largest possible number of Christians in the ministry and mission of the Church, and to prepare them for this involvement.

In the modern world such education is best carried on by other methods than the sermon—a relatively ineffective educational tool, since it cannot adequately be adjusted to the needs of different groups within the congregation, and it does not make possible adequate participation or response. Courses, conferences and group-work are needed as part of a systematic educational programme, which will require a wider base than an individual congregation. Christian education in the congregation and classes of instruction for church-membership do not give a complete and final presentation of Christian truth. They should point forward to further education at the adult level.

This further education should be comprehensive, and should aim at the education of the whole Church through all its members. It must go beyond the selection of an élite and the training of a professional ministry. Hence it cannot normally involve full-time study in an institution of higher education. What is required is rather a centre for Christian further education at the local level, offering part-time, evening and week-end courses, together with the occasional longer course. The establishment of such centres should be considered a priority by the churches. They should be fully ecumenical and should be owned and administered jointly by the co-operating denominations. Many such centres already exist, of course. What is new in this proposal, is the establishment of a network of such centres on a national or regional basis, sufficient to cover the total educational needs of the churches. This process will take time, but if these centres are seen as the basic institutions of theological education, and therefore as a first priority on the resources of the churches, existing buildings, funds and personnel can and should be diverted to them.[8]

The primary aim of such centres would be to provide theological education at the adult level for all Christians anxious to know more about their faith and its social and ethical implications, or desiring to equip themselves for Christian witness and service in particular contexts. The courses offered would also be open to enquirers. Church-membership would not be a prerequisite for attending courses, though churches and congregations might in due course wish to require attendance at such courses of new members or of adults seeking membership.

The centres might also be used for other purposes; for example for conferences on particular subjects, or on themes of current concern, for courses for vocational groups, for the study of local problems in a Christian setting, or for dialogue between Christians and others. They might also serve as centres for the continuing in-service education of ministers, and for some of the specialized courses described below.

As indicated previously, Christians who undertake a course of higher education at a university or elsewhere should be encouraged to study Christian theology as part of their course, where this is possible. Although the churches can no longer expect society to train their professional ministers through public institutions, they can demand that theology should be taught in the universities to those students who wish to study it. The Christian religion and that systematic reflection about it which is called theology is a significant aspect of human culture closely related to other disciplines. It is an objective field of study with its own laws and standards but using historical, linguistic and scientific methods. The churches should not expect such teaching to assume or require Christian commitment, and still less a denominational point of view; nor can they insist that Christian theology alone is taught. They should certainly not seek to keep Christian students from taking such courses in order not to expose them to other religious or ideological beliefs. Rather they should encourage them to enter into dialogue with students holding different presuppositions from themselves.

Only in those cases where public institutions cannot or will not provide for the study of Christian theology, should the churches establish parallel facilities in their own institutions where theology can be studied at the same level and with the same degree of rigour as in a university course. Such 'theological colleges' or 'houses of study'[9] should, however, be adjacent to universities so that students can reside in them or take courses there while undertaking their secular studies, or in the intervals of a university course. Care must be taken to see that the resulting time-table is not too heavy. These colleges, like the local centres just described, would be primarily aimed at Christians wishing to study theology at that level and at that point in their academic or professional career; but they would also have a part to play in the education of professional ministers.

So far in our plan we have been concerned with general theological education, so to speak, such as might be sought by any Christian and as may increasingly be regarded by the churches as a normal requirement. We must now consider what provisions are necessary for men and women called to exercise a particular ministry within the Church. Whether this ministry is part-time or full-time and hence, in that sense, 'professional', is not at the moment in question. Such persons will presumably already have followed courses at local centres of education, and in many cases at a university or in a university-related house of study. Three different groups can be distinguished with different educational requirements:

1. The first group consists of those with professional qualifications in other fields who offer their services to ministerial teams as teachers, social workers, or whatever it may be. Some of them may be entering church employment, others will fulfil their ministry in their spare time; still others may wish their professional work in government or independent employment to be regarded as a Christian ministry. In every case we can assume that they will already possess such professional training and qualifications as public authority may demand. If they have not already done so, they should work for a time in their profession before being admitted as full members of a ministerial team.

Where their intention is already clear at the time of their professional training, it may be possible for them to take a theological course at a university or in a house of study. This would include residence in a Christian community together with a basic theological course, which might alternatively be provided either before or immediately after their professional studies, or even during professional employment. Later entrants may be able to take a brief full-time course in theology; or may have to follow a longer evening and week-end course such as might be offered at a local educational centre in an urban area. In any case such a course should form an introduction to theological thinking with opportunity for reflection on particular professional problems, and, in addition, some specialized study as indicated below.

2. The second group will consist of those who have taken or are capable of taking a university course in theology or its equivalent. They should in addition be required to spend at least a year in a Christian community (not necessarily residential) for further study and group reflection on the life and mission of the Church, and including field education under supervision. Clearly where university studies are not a live option, the churches will have to provide a complete theological course for these students along lines suggested in Chapter 10; the main argument of that chapter will in any case apply to those parts of the course for which the churches are responsible (and indeed to the university course too where this is open to change).

Students of this group should be required, where possible, to train for another trade or profession in addition to the Christian ministry. In many cases this can be done before their university course; but where they have ability in another academic or professional field, they should be encouraged to pursue this at university in addition to theology, even if this delays their final qualification.

3. The third group will consist of those without higher academic qualifications and without the intellectual ability or attainment which would admit them to a course of higher education. Candidates of this kind were often, in earlier days, excluded from the Christian ministry, but churches today are beginning to realize that ability to take a university course is neither a requirement nor a guarantee of a call to Christian ministry. In Chapter 10 we have drawn attention to some of the experiments in planning courses for this kind of

student, especially for those who are somewhat older than the average candidate. Further experiments of this kind are much needed. Younger candidates should be encouraged to proceed as far as possible in their educational career, and if they are not able to gain university entrance to take other employment for a time and to follow an evening course as outlined above at a local educational centre. A further residential course should be provided for all candidates at a suitable stage; it should be geared to the educational needs of this group and should include a period of field-education. In some cases such courses might be undertaken by the same centres, though this will not always be possible or appropriate.

All three groups will also require some form of continuing education throughout their ministry. A regular scheme of continuing education might be based on the network of local centres. Specialized courses will also be needed for specialized ministries of different kinds, or for ministry in certain areas or with certain groups of people. These courses might partly be available at the universities or alternatively in the church colleges described above. Every possible use should be made of public educational facilities (including university extension courses) in sociology, psychology and related fields and in practical training[10] for social workers and the other helping professions.

It is impossible to describe in greater detail the kind of institutions that would be required to provide such courses as are here proposed. In the nature of things there will be great variation from case to case and it will depend to a large extent on what provisions for theological education are made by the universities or other public agencies. In earlier chapters we have referred to a number of proposals which might seem appropriate in different circumstances[11] but which are primarily intended to improve the education of professional ministers. On a wider view, many of the suggested improvements would also assist in the theological education of the whole Church, but by themselves they would not be sufficient. Hence the need for the establishment of a network of local educational centres serving the churches each in a limited geographical area, and backed by a carefully thought-out educational strategy.

The main conclusion emerging from this study is the need for such a strategy. Theological education is too piecemeal and too limited. If we are to take seriously the challenge of recent thinking on the Church and its mission and on ministry within the Church, we must grasp the bull by the horns and plan for an educated Church. It is not enough to abolish the distinction between theological education and laity formation, or to throw theological schools open to all who care to come. What is needed is a strategy developed by the churches ecumenically and accepted by them as the basis for their action and their planning.

Appendix

Official Report of the Study on Patterns of Ministry and Theological Education to the Fourth Assembly of the World Council of Churches, Uppsala, Sweden, 4-19 July 1968

A. *Introduction*

The Study on Patterns of Ministry and Theological Education was set up in 1964 within the Division of Studies under Programme Project procedures, in accordance with the request of the New Delhi Assembly to conduct 'a substantial Study on the Training of the Ministry in our time'. It was assigned as its remit the following questions:

1 'How can the work of the ministry be performed and new patterns of ministry be recognized and utilized in new situations of the modern world?'
2 'What modifications in the traditional academic curricula and methods of practical training are called for in order to meet the challenge of changing times?'

The Study has been largely conducted by means of regional consultation and study groups, and has dealt with the two questions in turn. Reports of these meetings and other documents have been published from time to time in the series of working papers entitled *Ministry*, of which seven issues have appeared. A final consultation including representatives from all the regional discussions was held in the London College of Divinity, Northwood, in July 1967. The recommendations of this Consultation, together with an Interim Report on the Study were presented to the Central Committee at Heraklion. This present Report, to be supplemented by a longer publication appearing later in 1968,[1] summarizes the conclusions of the whole Study and includes the recommendations mentioned above. These are addressed to member churches, to institutions of theological education, and to other bodies having responsibility in this field.

B. *Patterns of Ministry*

The discussion on Patterns of Ministry has considered the following topics, which are reported in detail in *Ministry* I-IV:

a recent changes in the social role and in the popular image of the ministry, often resulting in discrepancy between the teaching and the practice of the churches;
b the variety of patterns of ministry in the history of the Church, and in different parts of the world today;
c the rise of specialized ministries—their character and distribution and their relationship with each other and with the parish ministry;
d the ordained ministry as related to the laity and to other professional or voluntary diaconal ministries in the Church;
e certain new and flexible forms of ministry, and notably experiments in team ministry;
f experiments in non-professional or 'tent-making' ministry;
g the shortage of ministerial candidates.

If we take into account the purpose of this study—to examine theological education in the light of actual and desirable changes in patterns of ministry—we can regard the work that has been done as sufficient to allow us to make a number of points, as stated briefly below. This should not blind us to the fact that further research is urgently required if the churches are to develop a coherent pastoral and missionary strategy. If and when this is undertaken there may well be further implications for theological education in addition to those we can see at the moment.

Points of Agreement

1. The predominance of the pastoral concept of the ministry in recent church history has tended to give the impression that the minister is the functionary of an institution he is employed to maintain. A missionary understanding of the Church requires a more flexible concept of the ministry, and one that is world-directed instead of merely church-directed.

2. Although there is great diversity in patterns of ministry, it is a geographical and sociological diversity and not a denominational one. Churches working in the same area tend to develop similar patterns of ministry, regardless of their theological presuppositions. In working out new forms of ministry, joint action is common; it should also be the rule in maintaining and transforming traditional ones.

3. In the complex and pluralistic society of today, no single pattern of ministry can ensure that the Church's witness is made at every point, and that every social group receives adequate pastoral care. A comprehensive strategy is required making use of specialized ministries but always in conjunction with the pastoral ministry to communities of various kinds.

4. The isolation of ministers from each other and from the laity has in the past been a source of weakness and tension. Recent experiments in team ministry require further study. Where teams include ministers with different gifts, some of them perhaps in secular work, as well as laymen with professional qualifications, though not all in church employment, a ministry to larger communities becomes possible and also a more effective missionary outreach. Such teams also provide the pastoral care and spiritual discipline for their members which other patterns of ministry often fail to supply.

5. There is also a need for further experiments of new and flexible patterns of ministry adapted to situations hitherto unexplored. Further study is required of non-professional or tent-making ministry both in the industrial West and in scattered communities in non-Christian lands. The study of tent-making ministry is of particular interest because it enables us to free our concept of the ministry from its connection with outworn or inappropriate sociological categories in Africa and Asia as well as in Europe and North America.

Ministry and Laity

6. In the discussion on the ministry two views are represented which may be expressed as follows: (a) the minister is a layman trained and appointed to do a particular job, which is often admittedly ill-defined, but which is in general concerned with *equipping* the other members of the Church; and (b) the minister has the function, distinguishing him from the layman, of *representing* Christ in his Church—a function most clearly seen when he celebrates the sacraments, proclaims the Word of God or exercises pastoral rule in the congregation. These views are not necessarily incompatible; the discussion on ordination proposed by the Faith and Order Commission may serve to reconcile them.

In starting our consideration of patterns of ministry from the work of ordained ministers we were faced with a difficulty, since churches give different answers to the question: who should be ordained? Whatever importance is attached to ordination, it seems clear that the ministry of those who are ordained should be thought of in the light of Christ's ministry which he has given his whole Church, and in relation to the different ministries of other church members. In recruiting candidates for the ministry and in planning theological education, there is need for greater clarity on the part of the churches regarding the function of ordained ministers in the life and mission of the Church, and the relation between their ministry and the ministry of the laity.

C. *Theological Education*

Theological Education is usually considered to be the process of training ministers to work as pastors or theologians in a particular church. This training has three aspects:

a *academic education*, often carried on in university institutions outside church control, and aimed at imparting certain proficiency in the classical disciplines: OT, NT, Systematic Theology, Church History and Practical Theology;

b *practical training*, frequently including periods of field-work in parish situations or elsewhere, consisting of practice in preaching, teaching conducting worship and pastoral care;

c *spiritual formation*, usually in the context of a residential community, and aiming at the spiritual and devotional preparation of ordinands to be men of God, and to be pastors and priests to other Christians.

The present ecumenical situation, the current ecumenical debate on the Nature and Mission of the Church, and the foregoing study on Patterns of Ministry, combine to show up the inadequacy of this view. In effect, most existing programmes of theological education are designed for the training of professional ministers for a pastoral ministry in churches which are static, introverted and institutional, and which intend to remain divided.

In the terms of this Study, Theological Education must be seen as more than just 'training for the ordained ministry'. This function, indeed, is only one part of the total educational responsibility of the Church: to enable each and every member of the Church to go as far as possible in response to God's mission in Christ. Current distinctions between 'Christian Education' and 'Theological Education', between 'Ministerial Training' and 'Laity Formation', may have their practical value; they cannot, in the last resort, be theologically justified. This study is specifically concerned with the theological education of church leaders, including ministers and clergy, but it is important to stress at the start the *wholeness* of theological education.

It is certainly not intended to suggest that existing institutions of ministerial training are the best places for laity formation to take place (in some cases, the reverse might be nearer the truth). Rather it should be emphasized that the principles discerned here in theological education (as normally conceived) apply—as do also many of the practical points made—in the wider context which might, with equal justification, be known by that name. Theological Education, like Ministry, forms a whole much wider than that which has been traditionally understood by this term. Within the unity of Ministry, new forms of ministry, leadership and presence are emerging in the Church alongside the forms we know. Within the unity of Theological Education three strands may be distinguished which, it should be noted, do not correspond to the three traditional aspects listed above.

1. *The pursuit of truth with an enquiring mind and the honest facing of honest questions.* Theology is not merely to be regarded as information and instruction, but as a process of exploration and rediscovery. It includes openness to what God is saying in the turmoil of contemporary events. It includes search for the truth in dialogue with non-Christians. A necessary presupposition is an existential commitment to search for the truth with rigour and discipline, and with integrity of mind.

2 *The apprehension of the meaning of the Gospel as it is experienced in the confessing communities of the Church which responds to Christ.* Theology here is understood as that understanding of God's work and mission which goes with 'spiritual formation' of the individual Christian, and the building up of the Body of Christ. This element in theological education demands some kind of participation in a committed community.

3 *The vocational or functional formation of candidates for leadership roles and specialized ministries.* These are likely to become more diversified.

This insistence on the necessary strands in theological education in no way prejudges the structure of theological education or the parts played by university and seminary for the ordinand or ministerial candidate. At this stage we may note that the study of theology in a university is not merely an intellectual process, but requires personal involvement in the course, and in the wider life of the learning community; whereas a seminary can assist emotional development and growth to maturity, in a community which seeks to live by the Gospel. We note also that while, particularly in the later stages of ministerial training, a seminary community may be an appropriate base, much of this training will be done in other institutions; but all such vocational training should be related to the missionary tasks of the Church in the world.

The committed Christian who is *not* ordained expects, and is right to expect, from any course of theological education the same elements that are required in ministerial training. (1) He should be taught to pursue rigorously the question of truth. (2) He is right to expect theology to be related to the mission and life of the Church as well as to contemporary society; and he will hope to receive some spiritual formation by participation in a committed community. (3) He is also right to expect that he should be equipped for any ministry to which he is called.

The preceding paragraph (and Recommendation 1 below) has its primary reference to the trend, observable in North America and elsewhere, where large numbers of laymen are seeking some kind of theological education at institutions of university level, but without any specific professional orientation and often without clear Christian commitment. Theological schools in these areas are well aware of the challenge posed by this trend to traditional structures, and, on the whole, would welcome it as forming one element of the changing situation facing theological education today. The three strands, distinguished above, certainly apply here; but it may also be considered that they apply to other forms, and at other levels, of the Church's education (whether they be termed 'theological' or not)—and perhaps even at the congregational level.

D. *Recommendations of the Northwood Consultation*

I. Recommendations on General Policy

1. The planning of courses of theological education for ministers and laity should be related and co-ordinated as far as possible. Though circumstan-

ces will often dictate that the education of ministers should be done in separate institutions, shared courses should be the rule, where there is a comparable level of educational capacity. Even where courses are distinct, there is no reason why ministerial education should always take place in separate institutions from which lay persons are totally excluded.

2. Theological education for the ordained ministry has a 'professional' aspect, but the 'professional' training required may well overlap with that needed for professional church workers who are not ordained. The emergence of flexible and specialized ministries suggests that as much as possible of this training should be common to both groups. Churches are urged to study ways of co-ordinating their training programmes at this point, with a view to ensuring an adequate preparation for team ministry in the Church. Both pastors and other church workers should be trained to co-operate with lay people within the total ministry of the Church.

3. Joint planning and action for theological education is demanded alike by our common calling and our common situation today, as also by the developing co-operation between the churches. Ecumenical education, in which teachers and students of different church traditions join in the common task, is an instrument of great value in the actual processes of theological thinking and learning. Denominational schools and church programmes should take steps to plan for a co-ordinated or united theological education, while providing at the same time for any special confessional instruction or training that their churches require.

4. Theology should be studied and theological education given in continuous dialogue with the contemporary world, in such areas as:

a the understanding and communication of the faith in response to new insights about the world (particularly in the development of the natural sciences);
b the response to contemporary discussion about man and his problems (in philosophy, psychology, art and literature etc.);
c the understanding of social change;
d dialogue with men of other faiths.

Theological teachers must themselves be involved in this dialogue so as to be able to equip their students to judge the given situation and relate the Gospel to it, in an age when the given situation is constantly changing.

5. In theological education continuous research is required, including:

a theological research in relation to contemporary questions;
b sociological research into the structures of the church and its own training programmes;
c research in educational methods.

II. Recommendations on the Theological Curriculum

6. No single curriculum could fit the many situations in which theological education is being carried on today, but certain basic principles will affect curriculum planning in every theological school. All theological curricula must be planned in terms of the nature of theology (as outlined above); the functional purpose of theological education as preparation for ministry within the reconciling ministry of God; and the particular social, cultural, religious and educational context of the individual church or school. The whole curriculum should be rethought on this theological, functional and contextual basis.

7. One particular suggestion for such a restructuring is the thematic approach which builds a curriculum around a particular theme, e.g. 'The People of God, the World and Ministry'.

8. Full scope should be given to education for diversified ministries, by the provision of a common basic curriculum followed by appropriate specialized courses or by the use of specialized training facilities in other institutions. Further study is required on the content and structure of such a 'common basic curriculum' and on the point at which specialization is best introduced.

9. An adequate theological education should cover a period of at least 5 or 6 years, if it is to take into account the student's whole educational and vocational 'career' which begins at the point he attempts to decide what he will study and where, and ends when he is formally recognized in his chosen profession. This period need not all be spent at one theological school; there are considerabe advantages in a transfer to another institution, perhaps for the last one or two years, particularly if it has facilities for specialization in the area of the student's own interest.

10. The rethinking of the theological curriculum does not imply its ever

increasing expansion to a point which is beyond the capacity of the average student. It is imperative that drastic cuts should be made in the quantity of material which the student has to master for examinations, and that clear priorities should be established in what is to be learnt, both as regards which subjects are included in a basic curriculum and which kept over for later specialized courses, and as regards the amount of detail contained in each subject. In general, survey courses stressing the scope and significance of a particular subject should precede detailed treatment.

III. Recommendations on Structures and Relationships

11. Relationships between theological schools and universities should be established or strengthened where they already exist, and every use should be made of the educational resources which the universities provide. Theological study at a university should, however, be supplemented by additional training for those students preparing for the Christian ministry.

12. The size of a school must be related to the educational facilities available. A small school can be justified only if it can provide a proper variety of courses, a balanced educational programme, and a healthy diversity of experiences and viewpoints among teachers and students. Even when small schools are led to a merger (which in general is to be recommended) advantage should always be taken of the resources of a university or other centre of education if these are available. Large schools, on the other hand, must take appropriate steps to provide personal attention for students and to create smaller communities within the school in which a student can feel at home.

13. A significant portion of theological education should be conducted through involvement in social structures, by means of an urban training centre, an in-service programme, a year in industry etc. or other such means. Theological education ought also to be undertaken wherever the theological task is being pursued in novel forms by pioneering leaders and experimental projects unrelated to the established structures of theological education. Adequate professional supervision will, however, be necessary to allow for the creative involvement of students in projects of this kind.

14. Consideration should be given to the development of institutions specializing in the training for particular kinds of ministry.

15. The need for continuing study after ordination should also be kept in mind. Churches should ensure that provisions for continuing education are made and that these are related to the tasks and work of the ministry.

IV. Recommendations on Theological and Educational Standards

16. A theological school, like other educational institutions, must be characterized by integrity, openness to truth and academic rigour—whatever educational requirements it may demand or provide. It should therefore be prepared to enter into a critical relationship with the surrounding educational system, whether by relationship to a university or by other means.

17. It must equally meet standards derived from the faith of the Church as professed by the church or churches to which it is related and to the needs of these churches.

18. To become effective, the standards derived from both these sources must be freely accepted in mutual discussion with other theological schools of the same or other churches in the area. Manifestly standards of this kind can only be maintained by the discipline of a free and voluntary association.

19. Theological schools should examine their admission standards in the light of the educational system as a whole. Although in some areas university graduation is a normal requirement for ordination, or even for admission to a theological school, no universal standard can be laid down either for entry upon a theological course or for the completion of it. In some cases the theological school may have to set standards believed to be higher than those current in the educational system.

20. Standards should be set and maintained for the selection and education of teaching staff, including the provision of education in the art and technique of teaching.

21. Theological schools and programmes should adopt procedures for regular evaluation of their aims, curricula, methods of teaching and learning, systems of examination, financial support, quality of corporate life and effectiveness in relation to stated aims. Such procedures should include systematic internal study involving both students and teacher as well as inspection by external educational agencies and should make use of empirical methods where appropriate.

Appendix

V. Recommendations on Educational Methods

22. Since the centre of theological education is the student and not the teacher, careful attention must be paid to the qualifications, abilities and expectations of each student, and to the provision of an appropriate learning environment within which the student can mature as a Christian and can discover his place in the world and in the Church. Teaching must be student-oriented rather than teacher-dominated.

23. Teaching methods should be employed appropriate to the subject-matter and to the capabilities of teacher and students. In addition to lectures and seminars, these might include discussion groups, independent study, case-study, team teaching, student-directed study, and, where available, the use of technical aids such as language-laboratories, tape recorders, closed circuit TV. Students should be given ample opportunity to test their own ability to formulate and communicate what they are learning.

24. Provision should be made for supervision by qualified supervisors both in academic studies and in the practice of ministry as well as of the student's whole course in relation to his aims and abilities, the resources available and the demands of the church's task in the area.

25. Learning situations should be provided within which the student can learn to co-operate with his colleagues in the ministry, both ordained and lay, and with members of other professions, other churches and other faiths. Such situations might include hospitals, prisons, youth camps, industrial missions, village communities, adult education, urban training centres, projects relating to migration, refugees, immigrants, etc.

VI. Recommendations on Learning in Community

Some theological students still come to their studies with a firm, if immature, faith to seek professional preparation for the ministry, often on the basis of a strong and traditional Christian conviction, which often has to be held in the midst of a hostile society. In those areas, however, which are deeply affected by modern science and technology, many of those who come have radical questions about the truth of the Christian faith. Instead of seeking a more profound understanding and professional or academic expertise, today an increasing number are coming to theological schools to seek the very basics of the faith. While this shift has not taken place all over the world, and is quite absent in some countries, it is

160

likely to increase in extent and intensity. It is this trend which forms the background to the following recommendations.

26. Although in some traditions particular institutions may properly require prior commitment to the Christian faith of those entering a theological school, in many cases all that can be assumed is a desire to enquire concerning the truth and relevance of the faith. Curricula and educational methods must therefore be designed for enquirers. Questioning, probing, testing, experimenting are normal and proper approaches. The doors of the seminary must be open, even though this may mean severe tension between commitment to the Christian faith and an openness which enables real dialogue, and identification with contemporary doubts and questions.

27. In theological education the community plays an essential part since Christian theology is (1) like any other discipline of learning a corporate endeavour involving dialogue with scholars of other disciplines as well as with the larger community; and (2) an existential enterprise, deeply rooted in the faith of the Church. The student must be given freedom to discover his own identity as a Christian and his place in the Church by learning to use the tools of knowledge and the tradition and wisdom of the community under the guidance of a teacher, and together with his peers.

28. The common work of a theological school further requires some common discipline, and some common responsibility of students and teachers alike for the shape and functioning of the institution itself and for the larger world of which it is part. This can either take the form of individual involvement or of a common project of witness or service.

29. The life of the community is realized in many ways, formal and informal, and at different levels. Where the theological school is a residential community its life is frequently enriched by the presence of students from other academic disciplines and other church traditions.

30. It is desirable that all theological education should include a period, however limited, in a residential community. The problems of married students must, however, be taken into account, and provision be made for welcoming their wives and families into the community. In certain cases the community of the theological school can be built on this basis, and residential accommodation provided for married students and their wives.

31. The experience of several theological schools suggests that a valuable educational method consists in dividing students into small groups or '*équipes*' which may form units of study and field education as well as of fellowship and mutual care. In addition to counteracting the disadvantages of the larger school, this device can form an appropriate training for later participation in a team ministry.

32. An essential factor in community is common worship. Some traditions would emphasize the need to be rooted in the eucharistic worship of the Church. But in any tradition, small groups should be allowed to develop spontaneous and appropriate forms of worship. In a school which represents several denominations, the worship often gains from its ecumenical character.

33. Beyond the confines of the theological school, students may discover other types of community through participation in field education or internship programmes. In these cases the basis of community is not common residence but a shared involvement in a specific task or area of concern.

34. The aim of the entire educational process is the personal development of the student as a Christian. This spiritual formation is not limited to the period spent in a theological school, but it is a major responsibility of the school to co-ordinate all its resources towards this aim and to assist the student to discover for himself what his obedience means. He must be trusted in this personal search, but not left to his own resources; his fellow students as well as his teachers are engaged in the same search. He needs to learn what it means to live with others in the fellowship of the Spirit. Growth in Christ requires a rigorous study of scripture and tradition and also involvement in the world. This involvement should not be limited to ecclesiastical activity.

35. The whole process of spiritual formation has received insufficient attention in theological education, and further ecumenical study is required. Reflection is needed on the student's participation in the ordinary life of worship of a local community; his meditation on the significance of contemporary events in a Christian perspective; and his learning from other churches and traditions of spirituality.

(*Work Book for the Assembly Committees*,
World Council of Churches, Geneva, 1968,
pp. 126-34)

Table I

*Categories of Specialist Ministers in West European Churches
with percentage in each category*[1]

	1	2	3	4	5	6	7	8
A. EDUCATION								
1. Theol. Ed. (training ministers)	8·8	7·4	4·0	6·2	17·5	17·5	13·9	8·1
2. Schools and Rel. Ed.	15·0	0·4	17·0	35·1	11·5	6·8	6·0	19·5
3. Universities (not training ministers)	5·2	5·0	0·6	0·3	7·4	2·4	—	3·3
4. Research and lay training	0·4	6·0	1·0	3·7	3·2	1·4	5·4	1·7
Sub-total A	29·6	18·9	41·9	45·5	39·6	28·1	25·3	34·8
B. PASTORAL WORK								
1. Armed forces	13·5	29·6	4·2	7·6	—	—	13·9	10·4
2. Hospitals and institutions	4·4	14·8	3·7	12·0	19·3	8·7	3·6	7·1
3. Prisons	1·0	6·9	1·6	2·6	0·5	—	1·8	1·7
4. Students	3·7	4·6	2·4	2·8	3·7	2·9	1·2	3·2
5. Youth	1·0	6·4	2·1	3·1	2·3	11·1	13·9	2·6
6. Migrants and other ex-patriate groups	1·2	5·5	1·6	0·2	3·2	1·4	—	1·2
7. Other special groups	—	—	0·3	1·3	0·9	5·3	1·2	0·6
Sub-total B	25·0	68·0	19·6	29·9	29·9	29·6	35·6	27·5
C. EVANGELISM AND COMMUNICATION								
1. Home and industrial missions	2·9	1·8	10·8	9·3	2·8	8·3	12·1	6·1
2. Press, publishing, radio, TV	0·9	1·8	1·1	1·5	5·5	6·8	5·4	1·6
3. Music, drama, visual arts	—	—	—	0·2	—	1·0	—	0·1
4. Telephone ministry	0·2	—	0·1	—	0·5	—	1·8	0·2
5. Other forms of evangelism	0·2	—	0·8	0·1	0·9	1·9	5·4	0·5
Sub-total C	4·4	3·7	13·0	11·1	9·7	18·0	24·7	8·5
D. ADMINISTRATION AND SERVICE INSTITUTIONS								
1. Church admin. (central and regional)	17·5	7·4	4·5	5·0	4·6	6·3	5·4	11·1
2. Church institutions	0·5	0·9	9·1	2·7	5·1	9·2	1·8	2·9
3. Religious societies	8·8	—	8·8	0·8	2·8	1·4	—	6·0
4. Ecumenical bodies	1·1	0·9	0·1	0·2	3·2	2·9	1·8	0·9
5. Service instns. or other agencies	0·6	—	0·8	0·1	1·8	0·5	0·6	0·6
Sub-total D	28·7	9·2	23·6	8·7	17·5	20·3	9·6	21·5
E. OTHER CATEGORIES								
1. Cathedrals, retreat houses, etc.	5·1	—	—	—	0·9	3·9	—	2·6
2. Religious communities	4·8	—	—	—	1·4	—	3·0	2·4
3. Miscellaneous	2·2	—	1·8	0·5	0·9	—	1·8	1·5
Sub-total E	12·1	—	1·8	0·5	3·2	3·9	4·8	6·5
TOTAL SPECIALIST MINISTERS	100·0	100·0	100·0	100·0	100·0	100·0	100·0	100·0

KEY
1 Great Britain and Ireland
2 Netherlands
3 Scandinavia (Lutheran Folk Churches)
4 German Federal Republic (Landeskirche)
5 Switzerland (Reformed Churches)
6 Old Catholic and Free Churches in Scandinavia, Germany and Switzerland
7 Protestant Churches in Latin Europe
8 Total—Western Europe

Table II

Number and Percentage of Specialist Ministers in US Churches and Percentage of Ministers Working Overseas

(compared with *total* active ministers, not merely those in USA)

Church	Specialist Ministers No.	%	Ministers Overseas %
Seventh Day Adventists	14,968	58·6	—
Seventh Day Baptists	13	29·7	0·5
United Church of Christ	1,770	23·8	4·7
United Presb. Ch. USA	1,845	18·8	3·3
Christian Ch. (Disciples)	840	17·4	4·7
Presb. Ch. US	588	17·1	4·3
Ev. Covenant Church	92	16·7	6·2
Ch. of the Nazarene	683	15·2	4·5
Moravian Ch. in America	21	14·8	23·0
Lutheran Ch., Missouri Syn.	832	14·7	3·1
American Lutheran Church	729	14·5	4·4
American Bapt. Convention	895	14·2	3·4
Prot. Episcopal Church	1,204	14·1	4·6
Church of the Brethren	137	13·1	3·2
Southern Bapt. Convention	4,818	12·8	5·1
Evang. United Brethren	337	12·3	1·7
Methodist Church	2,882	10·2	1·2
Lutheran Ch. in America	620	9·9	2·0
Reformed Ch. in America	92	8·9	4·1

Table III

Activities of Post-War Graduates in Japan

	Pastoral	Educational Rel.	Educational Other	Professions Social	Professions Other	Misc.	Total
Men	1,828	59	161	33	252	144	2,477
Women	395	6	87	25	86	346	945
Total	2,223	65	248	58	338	490	3,422
%	65	2	7	2	10	14	100

Table IV

Activities of Graduates in Korea

	Pastoral	Theol.Ed.	Edcatnl.	Military Chaplaincy	Social	Secular	Misc.	Total
Men	1,238	25	255	74	56	232	352	2,232
Women	83	1	35	0	14	67	159	359
Total	1,321	26	290	74	70	299	511	2,591
%	51	1	11	3	3	11	20	100

Notes

INTRODUCTION

1 'Le Manifeste des "22" ', in *Bulletin du Centre Protestant d'Études*, Geneva, November 1968.

CHAPTER 1

1 Neither of my grandfathers had a telephone throughout the whole of their ministry, which lasted, in each case, into the 1920s.

2 See K. Rahner, *Missions and Grace*, Sheed & Ward, London and New York, 1964, Vol. 2.

3 See D. Webster, *Patterns of Part-time Ministry in some Churches in South America*, World Dominion Press, London, 1964; and C. Lalive d'Epinay, *Haven of the Masses, a Study of the Pentecostal Movement in Chile*, Lutterworth, London, 1969.

4 See the article by Olav Hanssen on 'A Dynamic and Flexible Form of Ministry', in *International Review of Missions*, LIII, 212, October 1964.

5 Dr. Philip Hammond of Yale considers that the mediaeval Church solved the problem of containing and using its radical elements by 'segmenting' them in monasteries. Specialist ministers are the 'segmented radicals' of today. See the Dudleian lecture by J. Edward Dirks, 'Specialized Ministries in a Diversified Culture: Confusion or Confluence', Harvard Divinity School, 1965.

CHAPTER 3

1 In *The Church for Others*, WCC, Geneva, 1967, pp. 30 ff.

2 *The Shape of the Ministry*, BCC, London, 1965.

3 See G. W. Webber, *God's Colony in Man's World*, Abingdon Press, Nashville, 1960; also Bruce Kenrick, *Come Out the Wilderness*, Collins, London, 1965.

4 The *Lettre aux communautés de la Mission de France*, obtainable from B.P. 38, 94-Fontenay-sous-Bois, France.

5 Arthur C. Smith, *Team and Group Ministry*, Church Information Office,

London, 1965. See also T. Beeson (Ed.), *Partnership in Ministry*, Mowbray, London, 1964.

6 CA 1640, *Partners in Ministry*, Church Information Office, London, 1967.

7 This is the main point of the current emphasis of the World Council of Churches' Division of World Mission and Evangelism on 'Joint Action for Mission'.

8 See Ross P. Scherer, 'The Minister as a Professional', a paper prepared for the Consultation on Patterns of Ministry and Theological Education, Washington DC, December, 1966; and J. O. Glasse, *Profession: Minister*, Abingdon Press, Nashville, 1968.

9 See for example J. E. Newport, *A Ministry Accepted by All*, BCC, London, 1964; Samuel Blizzard, 'A Minister's Dilemma' in *Christian Century*, 25 April 1956; Wurzbacher, Bolte, Klaus-Roeder and Rendtorff, *Der Pfarrer in der modernen Gesellschaft*, Furche-Verlag, Hamburg, 1960.

10 The value of such teams is not in question especially when their membership is fully international. The team recently sent into an unevangelized area of Dahomey by *Action Apostolique Commune* includes African, Malagasy and Polynesian members and is supported up to 45 per cent by French-speaking churches in those areas. But this is not a permanent solution.

11 C. H. Hwang (Dr. Shoki Coe) in 'A Rethinking of Theological Training for the Ministry in the Younger Churches Today', *South East Asia Journal of Theology*, IV, 2, Singapore, 1962.

12 Hans-Ruedi Weber, *The Militant Ministry*, Fortress Press, Philadelphia, 1963, pp. 38–9.

13 J. V. Taylor in *International Review of Missions*, LVI, 222, April 1967, p. 150.

14 See J. A. T. Robinson, Bishop of Woolwich, in *Meeting, Membership and Ministry*, Prism Pamphlet 31, London, 1966, p. 6.

15 In an unpublished paper entitled 'The Fulness of Christ; Perspectives on Ministries in Renewal', quoted by permission.

CHAPTER 4

1 From M. Rinvolucri, *Anatomy of a Church, Greek Orthodoxy Today*, Burns & Oates, London, 1966, pp. 20 ff.

2 From 'The Church Office in the Seed Store' in S. Crysdale, *Churches Where the Action Is*, United Church of Canada, Toronto, 1966, pp. 49–57.

3 From Donald L. Matthews, 'On the Docks of an African Port', in *A Monthly Letter about Evangelism*, No. 9, WCC, Geneva, December 1964.

4 From Kyoji Buma, 'A Church with Gas Fume and Bean Soup Smell', in *A Monthly Letter about Evangelism*, No. 4, WCC, Geneva, April 1964.

5 J. C. Barreau and D. Barbé, *Le Prêtre dans la Mission*, Ed. du Seuil, Paris, 1965, pp. 89 ff., reviewed in *International Review of Missions*, LV, 219, July 1966.

Notes

6 G. R. Dunstan, 'The Sacred Ministry as a Learned Profession', in *Theology*, LXX, 568, October 1967, pp. 433–42.

7 Philip R. Phenix in 'A Functional Approach to the Understanding of Ministry', a paper produced for the WCC Study and printed in *Theological Education*, IV, 1, Autumn 1967, p. 529

8 J. Freytag, in *New Forms of Ministry*, ed. D. M. Paton, WCC, Geneva, 1965, pp. 55–83.

9 *A Tent-making Ministry*, WCC, Geneva, 1965 (out of print). See also *The Ministry of the Spirit; Selected Writings of Roland Allen*, ed. David M. Paton, World Dominion Press, London, 1960; and *Reform of the Ministry*, ed. D. M. Paton, Lutterworth, London, 1968.

10 See R. Denniston (Ed.), *Part-Time Priests?: A Discussion*, Skeffington, London, 1960; and John Rowe, *Priests and Workers: A Rejoinder*, Darton, Longman & Todd, London, 1965; and *Lambeth Report* 1968, SPCK, London, and Seabury Press, New York.

11 *Presbyterorum Ordinis*, para. 8, 1965.

12 See the article by the present author in *Study Encounter*, II, 2, Geneva, 1966, pp. 64–70.

13 Op. cit., p. 8.

CHAPTER 5

1 P. C. Rodger and L. Vischer (Eds.), *The Fourth World Conference on Faith and Order: The Report from Montreal 1963*, SCM Press, London, 1964, p. 26. See also Per Erik Persson, 'The Two Ways: Some Reflections on the Problem of the Ministry within Faith and Order, 1927–1964', in *Ecumenical Review*, XVII, 3, Geneva, July 1965, pp. 232–40.

2 'The Meaning of Ordination', *Study Encounter*, IV, 4, WCC, Geneva, 1968.

3 See the booklet by L. Vischer, *Ye are Baptized*, WCC, Geneva, 1961.

4 In the report, 'Christ's Ministry through His Whole Church and its Ministers', *Laity*, 15, Geneva, May 1963, p. 22.

5 'New Patterns of Ministry in the German Democratic Republic,' in *Concept*, XII, WCC, Geneva, December 1966. For another expression of this view see the articles in *Risk*, I, 2, WCC, Geneva, 1965.

6 Hans-Ruedi Weber, *The Militant Ministry: People and Pastors of the Early Church and Today*, Fortress Press, Philadelphia, 1963, see esp. pp. 38–9.

7 Anthony Hanson, *The Pioneer Ministry*, SCM Press, London, 1961, pp. 154 ff.

8 See A. T. Hanson, 'Shepherd, Teacher and Celebrant in the New Testament', in *New Forms of Ministry*, pp. 16–35.

9 A similar concept of the ordained ministry is held by certain Free Church writers, notably Daniel Jenkins in *The Protestant Ministry*, (Faber, London,

1958), Robert S. Paul in *Ministry* (Eerdmans, Grand Rapids, 1965) and Kenneth Grayston in 'Ministry and Laity' (*Church Quarterly*, I, 2, London, 1968). See also the article by an Anglican writer, Victor de Waal, in *Theology*, LXXI, 582, London, December 1968.

10 J. A. T. Robinson, Bishop of Woolwich, *Meeting, Membership and Ministry*, Prism Pamphlet 31, London, 1966.

11 In an unpublished paper written for the Faith and Order Study on 'Christ, the Holy Spirit, and the Ministry'.

12 *Laity*, 15, p. 37.

13 J. W. Stevenson, *God in my Unbelief*, Collins, London, 1960, p. 122.

CHAPTER 6

1 At Hong Kong (1965); Dunblane, Scotland (1966); Seoul, Korea (1966); Northwood, England (1967); Bangalore, India (1968); Hamilton, Ontario (1968); Suva, Fiji (1968).

2 C. S. Song, 'Theological Education: A Search for a New Break-through', in *North East Asia Journal of Theology*, I, 1, Tokyo, March 1968.

3 See *Theological Education*, III, 3, Spring 1967, on 'The Significance of University Study of Religion for Church and Seminary'.

4 See the Introduction to the Northwood Recommendations, Appendix, p. 155.

5 Kenneth Grayston, *Theology as Exploration*, Epworth, London, 1966; see also J. McIntyre, 'The Open-ness of Theology', in *New College Bulletin*, IV, 3, Edinburgh, 1968.

6 Richard Shaull in *Theological Education*, II, 2, 1967, p. 293.

7 Daniel Day Williams, 'The Morphology of Commitment in Theological Education', in *Theological Education*, V, 1, August 1968, p. 37.

8 Hiber Conteris, 'Theological Education in a Revolutionary Society' in J. L. Gonzales (Ed.), *Por la Renovacion del Entendimiento : La Educacion Teologica en la America Latina*, Puerto Rico, 1965, pp. 121–2.

9 The phrase is taken from the masterly essay by Charles Davis on 'Theology and its Present Task' in J. Coulson (Ed.), *Theology and the University*, Darton, Longman & Todd, London, 1964, which maintains that theology today requires four conditions for its pursuit: (a) a university milieu, (b) study by lay people, (c) ecumenical structure and direction, and (d) an existential character.

CHAPTER 7

1 J. Tennant-Smith at the Consultation on Theological Education in Europe, Dunblane, Scotland, September 1966. See *Ministry*, VI, pp. 4–5.

2 See lectures given at Centennial Convocation of Episcopal Theological School, Cambridge, USA, by Kenneth W. Andrews, Merle L. Borrowman, David P.

Notes

Cavers, Peter V. Lee on 'Theological Education as Professional Education', published in *Theological Education*, AATS, May 1969.

3 See the article by T. H. Ham in *Theological Education*, II, 3, 1966, pp. 211–18. For a further and most interesting discussion of medical education today see *The Christian Scholar*, L, 4, New York, Winter 1967.

4 Owen C. Thomas, 'Professional Education and Theological Education' in *Theological Education*, IV, 1, Autumn 1967, pp. 556–65.

5 Keith R. Bridston, 'Form and Function in the Education of Ministers', in *Theological Education*, IV, 1, Autumn 1967, pp. 543–55.

6 'Functionalism in Ministerial Training', the Report of Task Group I at the Washington Consultation, December 1966, in *Study Encounter*, II, 4, Geneva, 1967, pp. 180–3.

7 Frank Lloyd Wright, in *Architectural Forum*, special issue, 1938, quoted by Keith R. Bridston, op. cit., p. 543.

8 K. R. Bridston, 'Theoanalysis: An Approach to the Problem of Professionalism and Piety in Theological Education', a paper read to the second Canadian Consultation on Theological Education, Hamilton, Ontario, 1968.

9 See *Recommendations* 22 and 26, Appendix, pp. 160, 161.

CHAPTER 8

1 See *Recommendations* 3 and 11, Appendix, pp. 156, 158.

2 The occasional working paper of the Study on Patterns of Ministry and Theological Education, *Ministry*, I, which appeared in March 1965, is now out of print.

3 See, in addition to reports quoted in the text, the series of studies published by the International Missionary Council (later Division of World Mission and Evangelism, WCC) on 'Training for the Ministry' in Africa, Latin America and the Middle East (the last two still in print and available from Geneva), and the recent report of the Protestant Episcopal Church, USA, *Ministry for Tomorrow*, Seabury Press, New York, 1967.

4 One such 'theological university' is Union Theological Seminary, New York, which now has a link with the nearby Columbia University.

5 The South-East Asia Graduate School of Theology now offers courses in theological schools in the Philippines, Singapore, Taiwan and Thailand.

6 *Doing Theology Today*, Second Report of the Theological Education Committee of the Advisory Council for the Church's Ministry, Church Information Office, London, 1969, p. 4.

7 As may be seen from the Statement of the European Consultation on Theological Education, held in Dunblane, Scotland, in September 1966: see *Ministry*, VI, pp. 17–23.

8 See the *Northwood Recommendations* 11 and 16, Appendix, pp. 158, 159.

9 See, for example, 'Recommendation on the Reform of Theological Studies', in *Study Encounter*, III/4, Geneva, 1967, pp. 24–9.
10 For a description of some of these experiments, see *Ministry*, VI, pp. 38–9.
11 See W. Herrmann and G. Lautner, *Theologiestudium: Entwurf einer Reform*, the memorandum of the Theological Section of the West German Union of Students (VDS), published by Chr. Kaiser Verlag, Munich, 1965; also the review of this project by Heinz Eduard Tödt, Professor of Social Ethics at Heidelberg, in *Pastoraltheologie*, 55, Jg., Heft 4, January 1966; English translation in *Ministry*, V, pp. 10–18.
12 See the description and discussion of several 'Cooperative Structures for Theological Education', in *Theological Education*, IV, 4, Supp. 1, Summer 1968.
13 In *Theological Education*, IV, 4, Summer 1968.
14 See Walter Wagoner, 'A Model for Theological Education', in *Theological Education*, I, 2, Winter 1965, pp. 90–5.

CHAPTER 9

1 Charles R. Feilding, 'Education for Ministry', published in *Theological Education*, III, 1, 1966, p. 235.
2 See *Recommendations* 4, 13 and 34, Appendix, pp. 156, 158, 162.
3 The Metropolitan Intern Program of MUST is described in the article by George W. Webber, 'Training for Urban Mission', in *International Review of Missions*, LVI, 222, Geneva, April 1967, pp. 173–9.
4 Keith R. Bridston and Dwight W. Culver, *Pre-Seminary Education*, Augsburg Press, Minneapolis, 1965. The report of the Curriculum Task Force is given in *Theological Education*, IV, 3, Spring 1968.
5 John B. Coburn, 'A Perspective on Preparing Men for the Ministry', Easter-Bedell Lecture at Kenyon College, April 1968.
6 'Education for Ministry', *Theological Education*, III, 1, 1966, Chapter VI and especially pp. 176 ff., 181 ff.
7 See the articles on In-Parish Pastoral Studies at Yale Divinity School by Russell J. Becker and Jervis S. Zimmermann in *Theological Education*, III, 3, 1967. Similar programmes exist at Harvard and at Union.
8 Reports of these two Consultations held in 1964 and in 1965 are available from the Department of Ministry, Vocation and Pastoral Services, of the National Council of Churches, 475 Riverside Drive, NY., New York 10027, USA. See also the special issue of *Theological Education*, I, 4, 1965. A further development is the formation of the Academy of Parish Clergy Inc. in 1969 as a professional association with a minimum requirement for membership of 50 hours continuing education a year.
9 The Lutheran Church of America is proposing to initiate a plan for an annual

two-week paid study leave for all its pastors with a continuing education programme to be paid for by regular contributions by congregations.

10 See the article by the Director of the Institute, Reuel L. Howe, in *Theological
Education*, I, 4, 1965.

11 C. Lalive d'Epinay, 'The Training of Pastors and Theological Education:
The Case of Chile', in *International Review of Missions*, LVI, 222, April 1967.
See also, in the same issue, J. Hopewell, 'Mission and Seminary Structure'.

CHAPTER 10

1 W. Herrmann and G. Lautner, op. cit., p. 91, quoted by H. E. Tödt in *Ministry*,
V, p. 12.

2 Dr. Shoki Coe (C. H. Hwang) in the *North East Asia Journal of Theology*, I/1,
Tokyo, March 1968, pp. 126–31.

3 'Statement of the Second Consultation on Theological Education in South-
East Asia', in *South East Asia Journal of Theology*, April–July 1965, p. 148.

4 'Theological Education in North-East Asia', in *Ministry*, VII, p. 16.

5 *International Review of Missions*, LVI, 222, pp. 164–6.

6 Josef Smolik, in *Study Encounter*, III, 4, 1967, pp. 174–5.

7 *Uppsala Speaks*, Geneva, 1968, p. 38. See also *The Church for Others*, WCC,
Geneva, 1967.

8 Keith Bridston, in *Theological Training in the Modern World*, WSCF, Geneva,
1954, p. 41; quoted in the article 'Ecumenism and Ecumenics', in *Study Encounter*, I, 4, 1965, pp. 186–8.

9 For an account of these various curricula and for the proposals of the *Fakultätentag*, see *Study Encounter*, III, 4, 1967, pp. 188–201.

10 See Peter G. Gowing in the Report of the Consultation on Theological Educa-
tion held at Warwick, New York, March 1966, by the Division of Overseas
Ministries of the National Council of Churches in Christ in the USA; H. J.
Margull in *International Review of Missions*, LVI, 222, *Theological Education*
IV, 1.

11 See James Ashbrook, 'Two Kinds of Learning in Theological Education',
in *Theological Education*, II, 3, pp. 197–202; *Pastoral Care and the Training of
Ministers*, Report of a Working Party, BCC, London, 1969, pp. 31 ff.; and (for
the courses at Lichfield) *Study Encounter*, III, 4, 1967, p. 199.

12 For detailed description of some of these experiments see *Study Encounter*,
III, 4, 1967, pp. 188 ff.

13 See 'Teaching the Biblical Languages', in *Theological Education*, III, 4,
Summer 1967.

14 Karl Rahner, *Mission and Grace*, II, Sheed & Ward, New York, 1964, pp.
166 ff., quoted by Bridston, op. cit., p. 554.

15 John V. Taylor in *International Review of Missions*, LVI, 222, pp. 145–57.

CHAPTER 11

1 See further on this point the article by the present author on 'Learning in Community: Spiritual Formation in Ecumenical Discussion', in *Seminarium*, No. 3, 1968, Rome, pp. 530–47.
2 See Walter D. Wagoner, *The Seminary: Protestant and Catholic*, Sheed & Ward, New York, 1966 (especially Chapter 2: 'The Catholic Seminary as Theological Oratory'); the article by Stafford Poole, C.M., 'Preparation of the Roman Catholic Priest as Person in Community', in *Theological Education*, II, 1, 1965; and the article by Bridston in *Theological Education*, IV, 1, 1967, p. 551.
3 See Appendix, p. 161.
4 *Ministry*, VI, October 1966, p. 15.
5 See *Theological Education*, IV, 3, 1968. Two leading theological educators in the USA are now experimenting along these lines: G. W. Webber, now president of New York Theological Seminary which is initiating its own version of the AATS Curriculum; and Richard Shaull of Princeton in the city of Philadelphia —see his article in *Christianity and Crisis*, XXIX, 6, 14 April 1969, pp. 81–6.
6 *Study Encounter*, III, 4, 1967, pp. 187 ff.
7 Ibid., pp. 185 ff.
8 W. D. Wagoner, op. cit., pp. 48, 53 ff.
9 J. A. T. Robinson, *Honest to God*, SCM Press, London, 1963, pp. 91 ff.
10 Michael Quoist, *Prayers of Life*, ET, Gill, London, 1965.
11 See Eric James (Ed.), *Spirituality for Today*, SCM Press, London, 1968, pp. 15–28, 41–55. See also the article on 'Lay Spirituality and Devotional Life' by Ian M. Fraser in *Laity*, 25, WCC, Geneva, July 1968.
12 *South East Asia Journal of Theology*, April-July 1965, p. 149.
13 See the article by C. S. Song in *International Review of Missions*, LVI, 222, April 1967, pp. 167–72.

CHAPTER 12

1 See *Central Committee of the World Council of Churches, Minutes and Reports of the Twentieth Meeting*, WCC, Geneva, 1967, Appendix XI, pp. 171–4.
2 J. V. Taylor deplores this in the Church of England in his article in *International Review of Missions*, LVI, No. 222, April 1967, pp. 145 ff.
3 The recent decision of the World Council of Churches to set up an Office of Education with three desks for General Education, Christian Education, and Theological Education representatives, is a step in the same direction.
4 *Northwood Recommendation* 1, Appendix, p. 155.
5 The Bangalore Consultation on 'The Role of Theological Colleges in Lay

Notes

Training', 8–11 April 1968. The report and some of the speeches are contained in *Laity*, 25, WCC, Geneva, July 1968.

6 As, for instance, in Brazil where one Presbyterian seminary amongst others runs an evening course in 'Theology for the People of God' and where the Lutheran Evangelical Church has enrolled 1,000 laymen in a correspondence course on 'The Christian Faith'. See the analysis of theological education in Brazil by Aharon Sapsezian in *Monthly Letter about Evangelism*, WCC, Geneva, Nos. 8–10, October/December 1968.

7 The preliminary statement to the Enugu Central Committee of the WCC in 1965 suggested 'that it would be well to recognize at the outset that in pursuing our aim we may in the end of the day find it impossible to say anything useful about the theological education of those who are called to enter the regularly commissioned ministry except on the assumption that the churches must provide complementary theological education for those whose ministry though of equal significance is of a different and complementary kind'. *The Ecumenical Review*, XVII, No. 3, July 1965, WCC, Geneva, p. 263.

8 This proposal is basically similar to that made by J. V. Taylor in his article in the *International Review of Missions* referred to above.

9 See the proposal made by W. D. Wagoner which is discussed in Chapter 8.

10 The Southwark Ordination Course of the Church of England is based on extension lectures in theology of London University supplemented by week-end conferences and by practical work.

11 For example, the proposals of the Resources Planning Commission of the AATS (*Theological Education*, IV, 3) or those of the Section for Evangelical Theology of the German Union of Students (Herrmann and Lautner, *Theologiestudium*).

APPENDIX

1 That is this present book.

TABLES

1 The discrepancies in the totals are due to the fact that they include numbers of specialist ministers not assigned to a particular category.

Selected Bibliography

Some Recent Books

J. C. BARREAU and D. BARBÉ, *Le Prêtre dans la Mission*, Seuil, Paris, 1965.

T. BEESON (Ed.), *Partnership in Ministry*, Mowbray, London, 1964.

M. BRAUN, *Reformation des Theologiestudiums*, H. Reich Verlag, Hamburg, 1966.

K. R. BRIDSTON and D. W. CULVER, *The Making of Ministers: Essays on Clergy Training Today*, Augsburg Press, Minneapolis, 1964; *Preseminary Education: Report of the Lilly Study*, Macmillan, New York, 1964;

The Church for Others, Two Reports on the Missionary Structure of the Congregation, World Council of Churches, Geneva, 1967.

J. COBURN, *Minister, man-in-the-middle*, Macmillan, New York, 1963.

J. COULSON (Ed.), *Theology and the University, an Ecumenical Investigation*, Darton, Longman & Todd, London, 1964.

R. DENNISTON (Ed.), *Part-Time Priests*, Skeffington, London, 1960.

C. R. FEILDING, *Education for Ministry*, American Association of Theological Schools, Dayton, 1966.

J. O. GLASSE, *Profession: Minister*, Abingdon Press, Nashville, 1968.

J. L. GONZALEZ (Ed.), *Por la Renovacion del Entendimiento: La Educacion Teologica en la America Latina*, Puerto Rico, 1965.

S. L. GREENSLADE, *Shepherding the Flock: Problems of Pastoral Discipline in the Early Church and in the Younger Churches Today*, SCM Press, London, 1967.

A. T. HANSON, *The Pioneer Ministry*, SCM Press, London, 1961.

G. E. HARRIS, *A Ministry Renewed*, SCM Press, London, 1968.

W. HERRMANN and G. LAUTNER, *Theologiestudium: Entwurf einer Reform*, Christian Kaiser Verlag, Munich, 1965.

E. JAMES, *Odd Man Out? The Shape of the Ministry Today*, Hodder & Stoughton, London, 1962.

D. JENKINS, *The Protestant Ministry*, Faber, London, and Doubleday, New York, 1958.

B. KENRICK, *Come out the Wilderness*, Collins, London, 1962.

The Lambeth Conference 1968. Resolutions and Reports, SPCK, London, and Seabury Press, New York, 1968.

H. LEUENBERGER, *Berufung und Dienst—Beitrag zu einer Theologie des evangelischen Pfarrerberufes*, EVZ-Verlag, Zürich, 1966.

M

Bibliography

P. M. MILLER, *Equipping for Ministry in East Africa*, Central Tanzania Press, 1969.

B. S. MOSS, *Clergy Training Today*, SPCK, London, 1964.

H. NIEBUHR, D. D. WILLIAMS and J. M. GUSTAFSON, *The Advancement of Theological Education*, Harper, New York, 1957.

R. H. NIEBUHR, *The Purpose of the Church and its Ministry*, Harper, New York, 1956.

Pastoral Care and the Training of Ministers, Report of a Working Party of the British Council of Churches, BCC, London, 1969.

D. M. PATON (Ed.), *New Forms of Ministry*, CWME Research Pamphlet No. 12, Edinburgh House, London, 1965 (available from WCC, Geneva).

R. PAUL, *Ministry*, Eerdmans, Grand Rapids, 1965.

Presbyterorum Ordinis, Vatican Decree on the Life and Ministry of Priests, Rome, 1965.

N. M. PUSEY and C. L. TAYLOR, *Ministry for Tomorrow: Report of the Special Committee on Theological Education*, Seabury, New York, 1967.

A. M. RITTER and G. LEICH, *Wer ist die Kirche? Amt und Gemeinde im Neuen Testament, in der Kirchengeschichte und heute*, Vandenhoeck & Ruprecht, Göttingen, 1968.

J. A. T. ROBINSON, Bishop of Woolwich, *Meeting, Membership and Ministry*, Prism Pamphlet No. 31, London, 1966.

P. RODGER and L. VISCHER, *The Fourth World Conference on Faith and Order*, SCM Press, London, 1963.

W. SCOPES, *The Christian Ministry in Latin America and the Caribbean*, WCC, New York, 1962.

The Shape of the Ministry, Report of a Working Party of the British Council of Churches, BCC, London, 1965.

A. C. SMITH, *Team and Group Ministry*, Church Information Office, London, 1965.

J. W. STEVENSON, *God in my Unbelief*, Collins, London, 1960.

B. SUNDKLER, *The Christian Ministry in Africa*, SCM Press, London, 1960.

Theological Colleges for Tomorrow, Church Information Office, London, 1968.

W. D. WAGONER, *Bachelor of Divinity: Uncertain Servants in Seminary and Ministry*, Associated Press, New York, 1963; *The Seminary: Protestant and Catholic*, Sheed & Ward, New York, 1966.

G. W. WEBBER, *God's Colony in Man's World*, Abingdon Press, Nashville, 1960.

H. R. WEBER, *The Militant Ministry, People and Pastors of the Early Church Today*, Fortress Press, Philadelphia, 1963.

G. WURZBACHER, K. M. BOLTE, R. KLAUS-ROEDER and T. RENDTORFF, *Der Pfarrer in der modernen Gesellschaft*, Furche-Verlag, Hamburg, 1960.

Publications of the World Council of Churches, 150 *Route de Ferney, Geneva.*

Concept, Papers from the Department on Studies in Evangelism (relating especially to the study on the Missionary Structure of the Congregation).

International Review of Missions (see especially Vol. LVI, No. 222, April 1967, on 'Theological Education for Mission').

Laity Bulletin (see especially No. 15, May 1963; No. 20, November 1965; and No. 25, July 1968).

Ministry, Papers from the Study on Patterns of Ministry and Theological Education (I-VI duplicated, copies of IV, V, VI still available; VII is printed and contains the Report of the Seoul Consultation, 1966).

Risk, Bulletin of the Youth Department (I, 2, 1965, on 'The Ordained Ministry').

Study Encounter (see especially I, 4, 1965; II, 2, 1966; and III, 4, 1967 which contains the papers of the Northwood Consultation).

Other Periodicals

North East Asia Journal of Theology, quarterly review of the North East Asia Association of Theological Schools, 2-Ginza, 4-chome, Chuo-ko, Tokyo (I, 1, March 1968).

Seminarium, quarterly review of the Sacred Congregation for Catholic Education, Rome (see especially III, 1968, on 'Ecumenical Aspects of Priestly Formation').

South East Asia Journal of Theology, quarterly review of the Association of Theological Schools in South East Asia, 6 Mount Sophia, Singapore 9 (see especially the report of the Hong Kong Consultation, in VI, 4–VII, 1, April–July 1965).

Theological Education, quarterly review of the American Association of Theological Schools, 534 Third National Building, Dayton, Ohio, 45402. (Each issue contains valuable material on theological education; the papers of the American study group on Patterns of Ministry and Theological Education are contained in IV, 1, Autumn 1967; 'A Theological Curriculum for the 1970s' is contained in IV, 3, Spring 1968.)

Acknowledgements

•

The author and publishers wish to acknowledge their indebtedness for permission to reproduce copyright material as follows: from 'Spiritual Formation' by Georges Créspy in *Study Encounter*, III, 4, 1967, published by World Council of Churches, Geneva; from 'The Sacred Ministry as a Learned Profession' by G. R. Dunstan in *Theology*, LXX, 568, October 1967, published by SPCK, London; from 'The Ministry as a Profession' by Justus Freytag in *New Forms of Ministry*, edited by D. M. Paton, published by World Council of Churches, Geneva, 1965; from *The Pioneer Ministry* by Anthony Hanson, published by SCM Press, London, 1961; from 'Theological Education, "Missio Dei" ' by Josef Smolik in *Study Encounter*, III, 4, 1967, published by World Council of Churches, Geneva; from 'Professional Education and Theological Education' by Owen C. Thomas in *Theological Education*, IV, 1, 1967, Dayton, Ohio; from *The Seminary: Protestant and Catholic* by Walter D. Wagoner, © Sheed & Ward Inc., New York, 1966; from *The Militant Ministry: People and Pastors of the Early Church and Today*, by Hans-Ruedi Weber, published by Fortress Press, Philadelphia, 1963; from 'The Morphology of Commitment in Theological Education' by Daniel Day Williams in *Theological Education*, V, 1, 1968, Dayton, Ohio.

Index

Index

Africa, 105, 135
American Association of Theological Schools, 100, 105, 109, 122, 124, 127
Associations of theological schools, 92
Autonomy in theological education, 93 ff.

Bangalore Consultation 1968, 140 ff.
Baptism as the ordination of the laity, 58, 60, 62
Biblical languages, teaching of, 122

Case-study method, 80, 82, 87, 120, 160
Celibacy, 37, 135
Chaplaincies to special groups, 28, 31, 163
Christian presence, 50, 86
Church of England, 17, 36, 48, 73 theological education in, 97, 121, 131
Church of Scotland, 17, 64, 110
Clergy and laity, 10, 38, 41, 43, 58, 61, 79, 90, 152 ff.
Clinical Pastoral Education, 107 ff., 130
Community in theological education, 76, 125 ff.

Continuing education, 110 ff., 148, 159
in Europe, 111
in India, 112
in North America, 111 ff.
Curriculum, 114, 118 ff., 157 ff.

Dialogue in theological education, 75, 95, 127, 145, 156, 161
Doctrine of laity, 42 ff.
Doctrine of ministry, 29, 56 ff.

East Harlem Protestant Parish, 35
Ecumenical scholarships, 101, 107
Ecumenism in theological education, 75, 98 ff., 118
Election, 63 ff.

Faith and Order
Conference at Montreal 1963, 56
Conference at Nottingham 1964, 102
Study on Ordination, 57, 152
Fakultätentag, 118, 121, 123
Federal structures for theological education, 100
Field education, 107 ff., 148
Flexibility, 43
Flight from the parish, 9 ff., 27

Profession, concept of, 51 ff.
Professional character of ministry,
52 ff.
Professional or vocational education, 77 ff.
for business management, 82
for doctors, 81 ff.
for lawyers, 80 ff.
for teachers, 81
Purpose of theological education, 69

Religious studies in University
Departments, 71, 94, 96
Residential accommodation in
theological schools, 97, 135 ff.,
161
Rigour in theological education,
93 ff., 145, 159
Roman Catholic seminaries, 126,
129, 131

Sacrifice, 64
Sandwich method of theological
education, 121
Secular involvement, 104 ff.
Seoul Consultation 1966, 117
Service, 51, 86
South-East Asia, theological educa-
tion in, 116 ff., 133 ff.
Association of Theological
Schools, 92
Specialist ministers in
Europe, 26, 163
Japan and Korea, 27, 165
USA, 26, 164
Specialization in theological educa-
tion, 122 ff., 148, 157

Specialized ministries, 25 ff.,
151 ff., 163 ff.
Spiritual formation, 72, 131 ff.,
136, 153, 162
Spirituality Today, Conference on
(1967), 132
Strategy, 30, 149, 152
Student Christian Movement, 128
Supervision, 108, 121, 158, 160

Taizé Community, 34
Team ministry, 34 ff., 146, 151, 152
in different areas:
Africa and Asia, 37
East Germany, 59 ff.
England, 36
France, 36, 130
North America, 37
Scotland, 37
in New Testament, 40 ff.
Team teaching, 119
Teams in theological education,
130 ff., 162
Tent-making ministry, 53 ff., 74,
151, 152
in France, 54 ff.
in Hong Kong, 53
in South India, 53
Theologian, task of, 72 ff.
Theological awareness, 49 ff., 86
Theological education
as action, 76, 158
in community, 76, 125 ff., 161 ff.
as continuing, 76, 159
in dialogue, 75, 127, 156
in different areas:
Church of England, 97

185

Theological education—*cont.*
  Denmark, 97
  Germany, 96 ff.
  Latin America, 113
  the Netherlands, 96 ff.
  North America, 92, 100
  the Pacific, 96
  Scandinavia, 96
  Switzerland, 96 ff.
  the West Indies, 96
  as ecumenical, 75, 98, 118
  as existential, 75, 128, 155
  as functional, 84 ff., 154
  for mission, 116 ff., 154
  purpose of, 69
  in teams, 130 ff., 160, 162
  in the university, 91 ff., 147, 153, 158
Theological Education Fund, 69, 71, 120
Theological education of the whole people of God, 11, 69, 72, 73, 76, 137 ff.
Theological schools
  in Africa, 135
  in Asia, 118 ff., 120
  in Belgium, 131
  in Ceylon, 102
  in England, 98, 102, 122, 126, 135
  in France, 129, 131
  in Germany, 118, 135
  in the Pacific, 102

  in the USA, 74, 80, 92, 104, 118 ff., 123, 136
Theological students, 9, 128, 130
Theology today, 70, 72 ff.
Tradition in theological education, 129 ff., 132

Union colleges, 100
Universities, 91 ff., 145, 147
Uppsala Assembly 1968, 11, 117, 150
Urban training centres, 104 ff., 158, 160

Vatican Decree on the Life and Ministry of Priests 1965, 55, 57
Vocational education, 77 ff.

Women in ministry, 21, 26, 136
Work of ministers in different countries:
  Africa, 45 ff.
  Canada, 45
  France, 47
  Japan, 46 ff.
  new towns, 37
  Orthodox churches, 44 ff.
Worker priest movement, 54 ff.
World Student Christian Federation, 118, 128
Worship, 134, 162

Youth ministry, 31, 47